Wooden Gongs and Drumbeats
African Folktales, Idioms and Proverbs

Published by
Adonis & Abbey Publishers Ltd
P.O. Box 43418
London
SE11 4XZ
http://www.adonis-abbey.com

First Edition, November 2003

Copyright © Dahi Chris Onuchukwu

British Library Cataloguing-in-Publication Data
A catalogue record for this book is available from the British
Library

ISBN: 0-9545037-3-2

Cover Design   Ifeanyi Adibe

Printed and bound in Great Britain by Lightning Source UK

Wooden Gongs and Drumbeats
African Folktales, Proverbs and Idioms

Dahi Chris Onuchukwu

Other Books by Adonis & Abbey include:

Broken Dreams
By Jideofor Adibe (Fiction/ Town Crier Series 1)

The Making of the Africa-Nation
Pan-Africanism and the African Renaissance
(Politics/Political Economy/Political History)
Edited by Mammo Muchie

Nigeria and the Politics of Unreason
A Study of the Obasanjo Regime
(Politics/Political Economy/Political History)
By Victor E. Dike

The Challenge of Authenticity: African Culture
and Faith Commitment
By Jacob Hevi

Table of contents

Part 2
Idioms and Proverbs

Dedication

In loving memory of my late parents:

Eze Sir James Ekeledo Onukwue
The Uba II of Ubakala
and
Ugoeze lady Celina Chintua Onukwue
The Ugoeze I of Ubakala

Also for
Lois, Chukwuebuka and Ihuoma Onukwue
You make the struggle all worth it

Forward

My father, the late Eze Sir James Ekeledo Onukwue was made the traditional ruler of my clan, *the Uba II of Ubakala,* Umuahia, when I was about eight years old. Though grateful for the honour, he could not immediately leave his businesses in the city to go and settle down as a traditional ruler in the village. My elder brother, who could have stood in for him, was at that time in a boarding school. As the second son, I was asked to stand in for him in the village as the symbolic ruler.

As a 'kid king', I had to be around when the traditional council adjudicated on many issues on behalf of my father or rather in my name as my father's representative. One of my earliest and fondest memories of this period was of a particular member of the traditional council who was exceptionally gifted in prudent oratory. He did not have any formal education but it was unimaginable that any major dispute in the clan should be adjudicated upon without his active involvement. In public platforms, he was truly distinguished. He could talk for hours, using appropriate folktales, proverbs and idioms to lace his statements. He was often able to pass on his message effectively without directly blaming or excusing any of the parties in the conflict. I later found out that most good speakers and arbitrators in the village rarely spoke directly or bluntly and that they all had a rich repertoire of folktales, proverbs, idioms and wisecracks, which they aptly used.

I became therefore very interested in folktales, proverbs and idioms not only for their functions as the palm oil with which words are eaten but also for their entertainment value.

Folktales can be broadly divided into two parts – those used to convey notions of wrong and right, and those used to explain certain mysteries - the "how and why" folktales such as why the tortoise has a rough shell or why the frog has big eyes. Stories of the latter type belong to the genre of mythology.

I have, in writing this book, deliberately used the African oral narrative style. I have chosen my words and constructed my sentences in such a way as to make the African voice in the narratives very prominent. Obviously something will always be lost when stories like these are rendered in a foreign language. Hopefully, the narrative style and logic will compensate for that. If I have succeeded in making the reader to share in the worldviews, norms and ethos, which the selected folktales, proverbs and idioms espouse, then I have fulfilled the main objective of the book.

I am grateful to the Almighty GOD for His *sustained wisdom and strength while I was writing this book.* To the Ekeledo clan, I say: *Thanks a lot for being always there for me.*

To Pastor Mike, Ngozi, Gloria and Praise Nwanegbo, my spiritual elders and family in Belgium: *A good brother's house is never far in times of plenty and in times of need.*

To Pastor Tunde Oke: *Thanks for taking out the time to check on the sheep in your care.*

To Mazi Nwora Mmadu: *For supporting my dreams.*

To Endy Nwosu, Larry Orlans, Okey Ukaegbu, Chukwudi Akaleme, Tine Vanackere, Enuma Otti, Chief Francis Ahanotu, Joyce Brown, Benedict Mayuku, Friday Iyamu, Ahmed, Ken and Queen Oritz Emeboh,

Bella and all the members of the Nigerian Community in Belgium: *A big thank you for all the emotional support. With friends like you a man cannot ask for more.*

To all the members of the Redeemed Christian Church of God World Wide especially the New Life Assembly Antwerp Parish, Belgium: *Thank you for all your prayers.*

To John Ubah, Chief Mike Ogundano, Remi Mmaduka, Ahmed Balogun, Tony Lamtey, Father Sabastine Onah, Nini Okey Uche and other members of the Nigerian Embassy in Brussels, Belgium. *Thanks for being there for me.*

To the Old Boys of Government College Umuahia: *May we always shine as one.*

To The Igbo Union In Antwerp, Belgium: *A big thank you for all the emotional support.*

And to the African Child Organisation, Belgium: *Yes every child deserves happiness*

Chris Dahi
Antwerp
October 22 2003.

Part 1
Folktales

A
How and why stories

1

Why the tortoise has a rough shell

Once upon a time, there was a severe famine in the land of the animals. All the rivers had dried up. The trees had shed all their leaves. The leaves had all dried up and were being blown around by the dry harmattan wind.

All the animals were starving. The antelope, the deer and even the great elephant and other herbivorous animals were all walking around, very hungry and looking very lean. The lion, the tiger, the leopard, the puma, the cheetah, and all the carnivorous animals did not even have the strength to hunt.

The tortoise was having the worst time, as he could not move fast enough to get to the nuts and grasses before the other animals. He continued begging for food from the other animals, but no one paid him any heed, as they all were hungry and had barely enough to eat.

Though all the animals were starving, the birds were looking well and obviously feeding well. Every day while the animals were gnashing their teeth and scratching their heads on how to find something to eat, the birds would be chirping happily and singing melodiously from the tree branches. They flew about merrily and sometimes noisily.

Everyone wondered how the birds managed to be so well fed and happy. The sly tortoise could no longer bear this. So one day, he approached the dove, which held him in high esteem as a wise philosopher.

" Mr dear dove" he greeted

"Good afternoon uncle, how are you?" the dove replied.

"*Aha*, how can you ask me how I am, when you can see that your old uncle is dying slowly? Sweet dove; you were always such a kindly and gentle bird. I cannot imagine that you could have the heart to watch callously while I die of hunger. If I die, my blood will be on your conscience. I assure you," the sweet- tongued tortoise said.

"But I have no food" defended the dove, who was no match to the witty tortoise.

"Ha, if you have no food, how come you are looking so fat and chubby?"

The simple dove flew down from the top branch she was perching, and came near to the tortoise.

"Sorry uncle, that you have suffered so much, you see, we birds have our spirit king living up in the sky. So every day we fly up there to feast. We eat heavily and drink enough to last us up to the next day"

"*Aha*, dear sweet dove, can't you take me up with you while attending this feast. I promise to be in my best behaviour."

"Sorry sir, but it is not my decision to make, you will have to speak to the other birds too."

" I will speak to them. Ehm, dearest sweet dove, could you please put in a good word for me."

"I will do that uncle, I will try my best for you";

The tortoise later spoke to the other birds, the eagle - the king of the birds, the wise owl, the hawk,

16

the kite, the wren, the nightingale and the others. He spoke so convincingly and earnestly that the birds agreed to help him but on the condition that he behaved himself as the tortoise was notoriously mischievous. He swore by his dead father's grave that he would be in his best behaviour.

The following day, when the birds were to go for their feast, they decided to take the tortoise with them. The eagle asked each bird to contribute a feather for the tortoise. Each bird gave the tortoise a feather. They used the gummy sap of the pear tree to stick it to the tortoise's body, so that he could fly with them to the sky.

The tortoise practiced flying for a few days. He was very excited and clapped his hands happily. He thanked the birds for their kind gesture. On the day they were to fly with the tortoise the king announced that every bird should converge at the square by sunset, so that they would all go together as they normally did.

As they were about to disperse, the wily old tortoise said that he had a suggestion to make. "Why don't we all take up some fanciful names that we could answer up there in the sky? It will add class, glamour and excitement to these feasts."

The wise owl blinked, and asked the tortoise why he thought the mere adoption of new names would give the party extra grandeur.

"*Aha*, began the imaginative tortoise. "Imagine calling each other names like Flying Beauty or the Wonderful Wise One or the Flowers of the Air. The peoples of the sky will be very much impressed by our creativity." The other gullible birds were caught by this introduction. They were simple impressionable birds. Immediately they started choosing flamboyant names like Morning Wonder, The Beautiful Guest of the Sky and the like. The eagle was not interested; he just shrugged and flew away. If it made his subjects happy, then, "no problem," he said.

The suspicious owl asked the tortoise what name he was going to choose and he replied "All of you"

The owl frowned at such an uncommon and funny name, but could not find any fault with it, so he too scratched his head and flew away

By sunset, the birds congregated at their normal meeting point, the air vibrating with excited shouts of their newly adopted names. The tortoise was the first to arrive. In fact, he did not leave from there after the meeting. He had simply found a corner at the venue of the meeting, withdrew into his shell and slept under some dry leaves till the birds re-convened. A little after the scheduled time, the eagle arrived and they were ready to leave. The eagle flew ahead and the others followed. The birds circled the tortoise as they flew in order to give him extra support.

They finally arrived at the palace in the sky and were heartily welcomed. After they had rested, the entertainment began.

The hosts, as tradition demanded, first served kola nuts. After the blessing of the kola nuts, the tortoise asked one of the hosts: " Excuse me sir, but please who are these fine big kola nuts for?"

"*Ah Ah*, my friend, it is for all of you, of course" the chief host replied.

"Ah, thank you kind sir." The tortoise descended on the kola nuts and ate them all alone because the kola nuts were for "all of you," which was his chosen name for the trip.

Next the hosts in the sky brought different kinds of delicious fruits.

18

"Ah, kind of you all sirs," the tortoise grovelled, and quickly asked in pretended innocence: "But please who are all these for?"

"It is for all of you, of course." Again the tortoise descended on the fruits alone, since the birds understood it as being meant only for the tortoise, whose name, for the trip, was 'all of you'.

After this, different kinds of sumptuous meals were served, and each again was said to be for "all of you," which again meant the tortoise alone -or so he made the birds believe.

There were more fresh palm wine and other drinks, which were again given to "all of you."

By now the birds were all fed up with the tortoise's nonsense. The eagle was so furious that he quickly told the other birds they were returning home to earth immediately. He gave strict orders that any bird that had donated any feather to the tortoise should ask the tortoise to return it immediately. Consequently all the birds demanded and got back their feathers from the tortoise. The gluttonous and greedy tortoise was trapped and stranded in the sky. He did not know how to get back to earth. The sky king of the birds had already bidden them farewell and shut his gate.

The tortoise called the gullible little dove, and asked her if she would be so mean as to leave him stranded and alone in the cold outdoors of the sky. The dove was embarrassed. She explained to the tortoise that she could not help him because the eagle had spoken against him. The other birds meanwhile were all taking off angrily, mad at how the tortoise had used them. The dove was eager to fly off too, not especially happy to be seen discussing with the tortoise, given what he had done. Many birds shouted at the dove, asking her to leave the wicked tortoise there so that he would die of cold. Desperately the tortoise cried out to the dove, as she was about to fly off with the wren. The kind-hearted dove waited, pleading with the wren to wait a while so she could find out what the old but ungrateful tortoise wanted.

The tortoise then pleaded with the dove to tell his wife, Ani, to bring out all the soft materials like the mattresses, pillows, clothing, and such things in their house. The dove wanted to know the reason for such a strange message, but the desperate tortoise asked her just to relay his request to his wife. The dove agreed and took off with the wren.

The wren demanded to know what the tortoise wanted from the dove. The dove told her the tortoise's odd request. The clever wren immediately understood why the tortoise made that request, and decided to teach him a lesson. He told the dove not to bother herself, that he would deliver the tortoise's message to his wife. The dove was grateful as she had another important appointment to keep, on getting home.

The wren flew directly to the tortoise's house, and told Ani that her husband had asked that she should bring outside all the sharp and hard implements in the house. Ani was puzzled by such an odd request, but did it nonetheless. She brought out all their hoes, knives, pots, pans, grinding stone and every other hard object in the house.

The tortoise, from the sky saw his wife bringing out things, but the distance was so much that he could not see exactly the objects she was bringing out. Aiming at the things in front of his house, he took a dive from the sky.

When he landed, it was a big crash. The tortoise's shell shattered and scattered all over the place. The tortoise's wife, on hearing the loud bang and her husband's scream, rushed out, and seeing what had happened, began to shout for help.

Luckily, there were some soldier ants within the vicinity. They responded to the distress call with speed. They quickly gathered all the scattered pieces of the tortoise's shell and cleverly and masterfully pieced them together. But it could not be as smooth as it used to be. This explains the roughness of the tortoise's shell.

2

Why the kite carries chickens

Arewa was the beautiful daughter of a king. She had upset her parents because she did not want to marry any of the suitors that wanted her hand in marriage. Different types of suitors had come – rich princes, powerful princes, tall ones, short ones and so on and so forth but they were all turned down.

One day the king of the spirits heard about Arewa and how beautiful she was. He also heard how she had refused to marry any of the men that had gone to seek her hand in marriage. Because the king of the spirit world was very ugly, he went to the beautiful fairy and borrowed a beautiful body. He also went to the king of the birds and borrowed a beautiful voice. The following day he left the land of the spirits and came to Arewa's father's palace with a big entourage. He came with horses, bags of gold, silver and other precious gifts.

When Arewa saw the handsome young man with the wonderful gifts, she was pleased and made up her mind to marry him. In the night the young man sang with such a melodious voice as was never heard in the land. Arewa demanded to know who was singing with such a sweet voice and was told that it was the handsome young man that all believed was a prince.
When the king of the spirits proposed to her the following day, she immediately accepted. The

handsome king of the spirits told Arewa's father that he came from a distant land. Arewa agreed to go with him, joking that even if he came from the land of the spirits, she would go with him. After the marriage ceremony, the spirit king put Arewa on his horse and rode away to the land of the spirits.

As soon as the spirit king got back to his land, he went and returned the beautiful body he had borrowed from a beautiful fairy and also returned the melodious voice he had borrowed from the king of the spirit birds.

Arewa was astonished at how ugly the king of the spirits really was after returning all the items of beauty he had borrowed to camouflage his ugliness.

So afraid was she of such an ugly creature that she ran into her room in a bid to hide away from the spirit king – her husband. But the spirit king caught her and put her in a big cage in the village square. They brought a big pot and made a big fire. Then they put the big pot on the fire, and put water and other ingredients. They were preparing to kill and eat her. Arewa was screaming, struggling to free herself.

Then she looked up and saw the kite hovering over the land of the spirits. Arewa began, in desperation, to sing to the kite.

> *Oh kite, hovering over the living and the living-dead*
> *Oh go tell my Father*
> *Oh go, tell my Mother*
> *That Arewa their daughter is lost while looking for a*
> *prefect husband.*

The kite came closer, and looked. It saw the beautiful Arewa. The kite was very sorry for her. It immediately flew to Arewa's father's house, and told him what he had seen in the land of the spirits. Arewa's father, the king, was very upset. The queen, his wife, wept. The king promised the kite anything he wanted if he could bring his daughter back.

The kite therefore flew back to the land of the spirits. He hovered over the king of the spirits' compound, then snatched a piece of burning wood from the fire and dropped it on the king of the spirits' house. The house caught fire. The spirits ran up and down, trying to put out the fire. The kite immediately grabbed Arewa and flew away. It took her back to her father's house.

Everyone in Arewa's family was exceedingly happy at the rescue operation. Her mother cried loudly, tears of joy freely streaming down her cheeks. Arewa too was very happy that she was saved. The king was very grateful to the kite and asked him to name what he wanted as a compensation for saving his daughter. The kite did not speak, but continued looking at the hen with its chicken.

The king asked the kite if he wanted the hen. The kite shook his head in the negative. He asked him if he wanted the chicken and he nodded happily in the affirmative. And so the king gave the kite a basket full of chickens. As the kite was flying away with his reward however, one chicken fell off the basket.

To this day the kite still searches for the chicken that fell off the basket and therefore ends up carrying chickens whenever he sees any.

3

How the cow became man's property

In the beginning, all the animals lived in the forest. The sheep, goat, cow, dog, birds, antelope, and others - all lived in the great forest.

In a homestead, many months journey from the great arid sea of sand, in the region before the beautiful blue river, lived Rikku.

Rikku, the son of Sule and the grandson of Haruna was a farmer. He was a great millet farmer. Rikku was so famous that people came from far and near to buy his millet.

Rikku was a good man. He never cheated any of his customers. He talked to them, and provided them with carriers, donkeys and camels to carry their purchases to their respective destinations. Whenever he was asked the secret of his success, his answer was always: "Hard work and sincerity."

Rikku was a big millet farmer. He planted only millets and no other crop. He understood the seasons, the heavenly signs and the weather just like any great scholar masters his area of academic specialisation. He knew when to plant and when not to. He could also read from the heavens if the weather was good for harvesting or not.

Rikku loved his millet fields very much, and treated them as if they were his children. He was always in the fields, weeding or putting more manure to an undernourished plant or removing dead leaves from another. He knew every inch of his millet farmland.

He also knew all the animals and birds that visited his farm. They were all his friends. He knew them all by name. He talked to them as he talked to his plants. They all liked him too. The birds picked on the insects that spoilt and fed on his millet. Sometimes he also fed the birds some of his millet.

Rikku was a great flutist. Whenever he was in his farm alone, he always played the flute. He slept over occasionally in his farm. If he did, he would play his flute at night, and whenever he played, the birds would stop chirping and the beasts in that forest would listen attentively, enjoying the sweet melodies that flowed from the flute. Many of the animals would often come very close to him as he played and most would be lured to deep sleep while listening and enjoying the melodies that flowed from his flute.

Rikku had only one regret – he was not married. It was not because he didn't want to get married. He simply had been unable to find the right person. Most of the young ladies were more interested in his wealth than in him as a person.

Rikku was playing his flute alone one midnight. The animals and the birds were as usual sleeping around him. Suddenly he thought he heard his name. He stopped playing and listened attentively. Not hearing his name repeated, he concluded it might have been the wind blowing through the leaves that sounded like his name. As he began playing his flute again, he thought he clearly heard *Rikkuuuuu!* Rikku stopped playing, and began straining his ears to know who was calling his name in the dead of the night like that. Then he heard a little noise from the forest path that led to his farm. Turning, he saw a very beautiful antelope, its brown skin and white stripes reflecting beautifully in the moonlight.

Rikku was enchanted, he had never seen this particular antelope in his farm before, or any as beautiful as it was. He continued watching the antelope, as it came closer. It got to where Rikku was standing, and stood looking at him

Rikku stretched out his hand and touched the beautiful antelope, and instantly it changed to a very beautiful maiden. She had prominent brown eyes. Her mouth was small and almost round, her nose, straight and perfect and her hair was long and silky, like the mane of a young horse. She was tall, elegant and very beautiful. She was dressed in a long gaily coloured silk caftan with a wrap of a different shade covering her head and a pair of skin sandals on her feet. She had carved bone bangles on her wrists.

Rikku was astounded. He stood looking at her, not knowing what to do, until she said with a voice as melodious as Rikku's flute: "Rikku please play your flute for me."

Rikku did not need a second prodding. He sat down, cross-legged and bade the pretty visitor to sit too, and then began playing. He played his flute that night with such gusto, as he had never mustered before. The tantalising melodies oozing from the flute was such that even the wind stopped to listen and enjoy it. The moon stopped its flight across the sky and the stars dimmed in respect to such a melodious music.

That was the start of a long and romantic relationship between Rikku and the beautiful antelope-girl.

One night, the antelope-girl took Rikku to the enchanted brook, where fishes could talk. She showed him the magic tree in the forest whose leaves could cure any known sickness. She took him to different corners and crevices of the great forest, showing and explaining to him all the hidden wonders and mysteries of the forest.

Rikku, on his part, taught her how to play the flute. They were indeed very good friends, she with the wonderful voice, and Rikku with the melodious flute. Whenever both played together, even the heavens would stop to listen.

She told Rikku that her name was Halima. She was the daughter of the forest fairy. She also told him that no other human eyes could see her except his.

One day Halima asked Rikku. "Dearest Rikku, will you marry me?"

Rikku was lost for words. When he finally collected himself, he was trembling in excitement, with tears of joy freely strolling down his eyes when he said 'yes.'

That night, they were married.

All the fairies and animals attended Halima and Rikku's wedding. The guests gave them many wonderful gifts. That night, Halima transformed Rikku's little farmland hut into a mansion for them. She waved her magic wand and Rikku's millet farm was filled with millet stalks, each bowing down due to the weight of the rich millet seeds it was carrying. Rikku's happiness knew no bounds.

One month later, Halima announced that she was pregnant. Rikku decided to stay with her every minute. He was extremely excited and happy. Here he was, with a wife he loved so much. And now they were going to have a baby! What else could a man desire from life? Rikku's joy was complete.

One day, while Halima was outside the house enjoying the evening fresh air, Rikku was inside their house preparing a meal of roasted corn. After preparing the meal, he decided to join his wife outside. But his wife was nowhere to be found. He found her beautiful robe and her coloured headscarf. He also found her carved bone bangles and her elegant sandals. Rikku searched for her everywhere, but she was nowhere to be found. He called out her name several times and played her favourite songs on the flute. But Halima did not answer. Rikku was heartbroken. He wept bitterly. The animals and birds that were Rikku's friends were heartbroken too. Only they knew what had happened. Halima was a fairy. Her time as a human being had expired and she had to go back to the spirit world where she belonged.

Every day Rikku would stay in front of his house playing sorrowful songs and weeping for the loss of his beloved wife.

Rikku's animal friends decided to do something about what had happened to their friend. They called a meeting of all the animals. On the day of the meeting, all the animals gathered, except the cow, which had gone out to feed in the fields. She had told the animals that whatever they decided at the meeting, she would abide by it. So in the meeting the animals decided that they would give one of their kinds to Rikku as a condolence for his lost wife. Every animal present made a case for why he or she would not be the one to go and live with Rikku. Then the cow was called out, as was done to all the other animals, to come and give reasons why she would not be the one to go and live with Rikku. But the cow

29

wasn't there. The tortoise said he had seen her hurrying to the field and had reminded her of the meeting but that she had retorted that whatever decision was reached at the meeting would be fine with her. The elephant then suggested that the cow would be asked to go and live with Rikku and all the other animals supported the motion.

The cow was returning from the field when the meeting was just ending. She asked of what was decided and was promptly told by the elephant that the entire animal kingdom spoke with one voice and had decided that she, the cow, should go and live with Rikku. The cow tried to protest but the tortoise quickly reminded her of her promise that she would abide by whatever decision the meeting took.

4

How the sheep lost its horn

The sheep used to have horns, which were widely regarded as the most beautiful horns on any animals on earth. The sheep's horns had branches and flowers, and little bells that rang when she walked. The sheep was very proud of her horns, and she was always at the ponds and streams admiring the reflections of her beautiful horns. Her horn made her quite vain and foolish.

In one village of human beings, there lived a widow and her two children, Ababina and Durugbo.

Ababi, as he was called for short, was the older of the two children of the poor widow. Ababi was a rascal. He neither obeyed nor respected their mother. He always took delight in doing those things, which their mother asked them not to do. He also cherished leaving their home when the sun was in the middle of the sky. This was generally believed to be the time when spirits moved about. Wise human beings knew they had to stay indoors during this time.

Ugbo, as the younger brother was fondly called, was very different from his elder brother. He was quiet, respectful and obedient. He did whatever their mother asked them to do without asking questions.

One day, as their mother was about to go to the big market many, many hours journey from their village, she gave them instructions on what to do while she was away. She told them not to make any bonfire in the afternoon so that no smoke would come out of the house. She also asked them not to pound anything on the wooden mortar so that bad spirits would not be attracted by the sound. She equally asked them not to roast any snail in the only fire embers in the house as the liquid from it might put out the fire since fire was so scarce it could only be got in the land of spirits. Most seriously the widow told her two children not to leave the house for any reason. When she left she told them to shut and lock the doors of the house securely.

Shortly after their mother left, Ababi started fretting. He announced that he wanted to eat snail meat. His brother reminded him of what their mother had said before she left. But Ababi remained adamant. He wanted to kindle the fire embers and roast the snail. He also wanted to pound pepper on the wooden mortar. Ugbo tried to stop him. But Ababi got angry and insisted on cooking and eating his own share of the snail meat at that time rather than when the sun had set and the spirits had gone home. Not wanting to get into any arguments with him, Ugbo went into his room to rest and have peace of mind.

As soon as he left, Ababi gathered some dry leaves and dry palm fronds and rekindled the live coals in the fireplace. This caused a lot of smoke, which drifted out of the chimney. Without hesitation, he tossed the snails into the fire and started pounding the pepper, which he would use to prepare the sauce. Before Ugbo could come out of the bedroom to find out what was happening, the water from the snail had put out the fire. Desperately they tried to rekindle the fire but the coal and leaves were too wet. The fire had gone out completely. They did not know what to do, except to wait until their mother came back.

Ugbo went back to his room. But Ababi opened the back door and sneaked out to go and fetch fire from the land of the spirits.

On the way he met a spirit with two heads, which curiously asked him where he was going. He replied that he was going to the land of the spirits to fetch fire. The spirit urged him to continue further down the road. After walking for a while, he met another spirit, which had three heads. This also directed him to continue walking further down the road. After a while he met another spirit with many heads. This one invited him into the house, and asked him to sit down. The wicked spirit offered him some water. "Drink my boy, I know you are very thirsty after your long journey in search of fire."

A little lizard on the rafter made a little noise. Ababi looked at it and it shook its head for Ababi not to drink the water. But Ababi ignored the lizard and drank the water.

Again the spirit offered him food. "Eat these yams and cocoyams. They are deliciously roasted. They will make you strong and healthy," the spirit said with a rue smile. The little lizard again tried to stop Ababi from eating, but Ababi, who always liked good meals, again went ahead and ate the food. Shortly after finishing the food, he fell down and died.

The spirit rubbed his hands gleefully and laughed happily. He had killed a little boy that they would eat in the morning. When it was nighttime in

33

the land of the spirits, it was still noon in the land of the human beings.

When Ugbo discovered that his brother had gone out of the house, he was upset and afraid for him. Ugbo knew that Adabi liked food so much that he would accept any food given to him in the land of the spirits. He immediately set out to look for his brother. Soon he met the spirit with two heads. "Where are you going to little boy?", the evil spirit asked him. "I am going to the land of the spirit to fetch my brother, who went there to fetch fire but has not come back. Did you see him?"

The spirit directed him further down the road. Also he met with the spirit that had three heads. That one also directed him to continue walking further down the road. Then he met the spirit with numerous heads. As with Alabi, it also invited Ugbo into its house and offered him water.

" Have some water little boy. I know you must be very thirsty after your long journey." Before Ugbo could touch the water, the little lizard in the rafter made a little noise, like it did when the spirit offered Ababi water earlier in the day. Ugbo looked at the little lizard, which shook its head frantically, signalling to him not to drink the water but to pour it away when the spirit was not looking.

The spirit next offered Ugbo yam and cocoyam. Again the little lizard warned him not to eat. Again he pretended to have eaten it, but threw them away when the spirit was not looking. Then he pretended to have died. The spirit was very happy. "Two fat little boys to eat in the morning. What a sumptuous feast this will be!," the spirit shouted joyously. The evil spirit carried Ugbo to where he had kept the dead body of his brother.

The lizard came over when the spirit was not around and showed Ugbo the horn on the wall that the spirits used to wake up dead people. He also informed Ugbo that when the spirits were snoring, it did not mean they were asleep. It was only when they would be heard whistling through their noses that he should know they were deeply asleep. At that time, suggested the lizard, he could wake his brother up with the horn, and they could run away to their home.

At mid night, after the spirits had gone to bed, and were snoring loudly, Ugbo kept quiet until they started whistling through their noses. Then Ugbo got up, and taking the magic horn from the wall, he started blowing.

Magic horn, magic horn
Wake up my dead brother for me.
He did not drink spirit water
He did not eat spirit yam
He did not eat spirit cocoyam

Immediately Ababi woke up and the two brothers started running home with the magic horn. Not long after they ran off, the elf woke up, and seeing that the two brothers had escaped, fetched the other horn and started blowing.

Magic horn, magic horn
Blow the children to death
They drank spirit water
They ate spirit yam
They ate spirit cocoyam

Immediately Ababi fell down, dead.
Again, Ugbo his brother, blew his own, and he got up again, and they continued running home. This dying and rising continued between the two children and

the spirit until they got to the land of human beings when the sun was still shining. From there they could no longer hear the horn of the spirit, therefore Ababi did not fall and die, when the spirit blew its own horn.

The children ran into their house and locked the door. There they stayed until their mother came back from the market, and they told her what had happened. Their mother took the magic horn and hung it on the fence where the children could not reach it.

The sheep was passing by, without looking where it was going. Suddenly its horns got caught by the rope on which the magic horn was hanging. The magic horn fell down and the careless sheep stepped on it, and the magic horn that could wake a dead person up broke into pieces. This is why, to this day, dead people can no longer be woken up.

The gods were very angry at the sheep, and knowing that it was extremely proud of its horns, they removed them from her. This is why until today the sheep does not have horns.

5

Why babies can't talk

In the beginning, every one could talk, including newly born babies. It was a very interesting period, because babies always made people laugh. They often would call a dog a goat. Sometimes, if they saw a cow, they would say: "Mummy look at a big dog with big horns," and people would laugh. Sometimes too, they made people very sad by what they said because being babies, they did not know when to speak and when to keep quiet.

There was a law that forbade babies from being punished for whatever they said because it was accepted that they were not as intelligent as the adults, and also did not know how to lie.

The king had a wife. They had been married for twelve years but the queen had not given the king a child so the king decided to marry another wife, as they were both getting old. The king did not want to die without an heir. So he went to the king of a neighbouring kingdom to ask for his daughter's hand in marriage. The neighbouring king agreed but told the old king that he would not want his daughter to be made unhappy or sad in any way whatsoever. He loved his daughter dearly and would not want anything or anyone to make her sad.

The old king agreed to that condition and they had a very colourful wedding that befitted a king and princess.

The princess's father gave the old king a lot of gift, as dowry. The old king in return also gave his in-law very expensive gifts, and a lot of money as bride price. Everyone was happy.

Everyone, except the old king's first wife. She was very unhappy that the old king married a new wife. She did not want another woman to come and share all the beautiful things and gifts her husband, the king, had been giving to her.

When the new wife arrived, the old queen pretended to be happy with her. She welcomed her, kissing her on both cheeks and telling her how lovely she was. She said that the palace would look gayer with her around to brighten it up. But in her heart, she was planning evil.

The king had a very beautiful horse. He loved the horse so much that he was the only one allowed to ride on it. One day the old queen dressed up in the new queen's robes and stole the king's horse. She rode it to the forest and hid it there.

She had made sure that a baby lying down near the horse's stable had seen her robe but not her face.

Soon the king started looking for his favourite horse. The wooden gong was sounded and all the people in the land were summoned to the palace. The king gave an order that the horse should be found. There was an order that anyone found to have stolen the horse would be punished severely. Everyone was worried.

When the little child's mother got to her house, she summoned all her children and told them that the king's horse was missing, and that the king was angry. The little baby immediately said that it was the new queen who stole the horse. The mother hushed her, telling her to shut up. But the baby shouted louder. She explained that she had seen the queen when she took the horse away from the stable. The mother shouted at her to keep quiet immediately, that she did not know what she was talking about. The baby started crying and yelling. The neighbours heard her cry and came over. On inquiry, the baby told them what she saw. The people were frightened, because they knew that if they revealed the information, and it turned out to be lies, the king would have them all thrown into jail.

The women reported to the elders what the baby had said. The elders went to the king and told him what they had heard.

Immediately the king ordered the baby to be brought before him. When the baby was brought before the king, she said exactly what she had seen that day. The king had his new queen summoned before him. Again the baby repeated what she saw that night. The queen was very embarrassed. She of course denied any knowledge of the horse's whereabouts. But the king believed the baby's story, because babies were not known to lie. The great king was very angry with the new queen and ordered that she should be taken to the market square and flogged as a punishment. After that, the king took the disgraced queen back to her father, the neighbouring king, and said he was no longer interested in marrying her.

The young queen's father was very angry. He remembered what he had told the old king before he accepted him as a son- in-law. He asked his daughter if she had actually stolen the horse and she denied that. She swore by their ancestors, forefathers and the great gods of their land that she did not do it. Her father was convinced of her innocence. Her father believed the old king merely wanted to humiliate his daughter and his own kingdom.

He prepared his army and declared war on the old king. The two kingdoms fought a fierce war for many days.

Then one day an old woodcutter who lived in the forest brought the missing horse back to the king's palace. He told the king that he saw the old queen bring the horse into the forest and tether it there. He said that since the old queen did not come back for the horse, he had concluded that she had come to some harm.

The king was very embarrassed about what he did to his new wife because of his jealous old wife. He called back his soldiers from the battlefield, and called off the war. But the other king was still angry. His daughter was still unhappy. He insisted that the war must continue.

The old king consulted the elders on what should be done to compensate the angry king. The elders consulted the oracle. The gods knew that the reason for all the people's problems was because of the baby who said what was not true.

So the gods decided that henceforth babies wouldn't speak again. They poured salt water into the baby's mouth, and from thence, babies stopped speaking. This is why to this day, any time a baby tries to talk, water would start dripping out of its mouth.

6

How the catfish got a flat head

One day the rascally tortoise insulted the lion's wife. The lion was infuriated and called the tortoise to either come out for a duel or apologise to his wife. The tortoise felt that an apology to a woman would be a humiliation to someone of his social standing. So he opted to fight the lion.

Both the date for the duel and the venue were agreed upon. The fight was to take place by the riverside. It was of course one-sided and short. The tortoise just went into his shell, and the lion could not get at him. So the lion out of frustration just threw him into the river and went home.

In the river, the tortoise who couldn't swim that well, shouted for the fishes to save him. He yelled so much that all the fishes in the river gathered to rescue him.

They dragged him to the shore and dumped him there. After he had recovered his breath, the tortoise told the fishes how grateful he was for their help. He asked what he could do to show his gratitude.

They agreed that he would entertain them with his magical skills. The tortoise promised to make each fish grow twice its normal size. He also promised to make their scales radiate with exceptional beauty such that each would look like a mermaid. All the fishes were excited, except the catfish, which did not trust the tortoise. He had once overheard some land animals that had come to the river to drink talking about the exploits of the tortoise and how unreliable and ungrateful he was.

The tortoise told the big fishes that each of them should bring a large quantity of oil, while the small fishes were to bring each, a small quantity of oil. He also asked the big fishes to bring each, a large quantity of salt while the small fishes would each bring a small quantity of salt. Next, he asked the big fishes to go and fetch each, a big quantity of firewood while the small fishes were to bring each, a small quantity of firewood.

The fishes eagerly brought all these in anticipation of the magic from the tortoise, which would make each double in size.

After he had made the fishes to bring many more ingredients, the tortoise brought out a very large frying pan. He poured the oil into it and put the salt. He cracked two stones together and made fire, upon which he put the frying pan. When the oil in the frying pan had become very hot, he told the fishes to start leaping in.

They were all excited and started leaping into the hot frying oil. Each fish that leapt into the frying oil appeared to have grown longer and bigger, so the others were encouraged to keep leaping in. The tortoise kept urging them on, chanting some incantations and promising that their scales would get as beautiful as mermaid's. More and more fishes were eager to jump in. Of course they were all being fried.

The catfish stayed aside and refused to join the rush to jump into the frying pan. He was curiously observing the whole drama. When the tortoise asked him to get into the frying pan, he refused, saying that the pan was already overcrowded. He insisted that, until those already in started getting out, he was not going to get in. The tortoise cajoled him, but he refused. He taunted him that he was afraid and cowardly. But the catfish was not impressed. Suddenly the tortoise hit him with the hot frying spoon. The agile catfish dodged but the hot spoon caught him on the head, scalding it, and flattening it too. The catfish quickly disappeared into the deeper water. That is why, until this day, the catfish has a flat and smooth shiny head.

7

Why mosquitoes buzz around the ear

The mosquito was a very presumptuous insect. He had a highly inflated idea of himself. The irony however was that he was so little that almost nobody took any notice of him. He was often cajoled for looking very tiny, sickly and emaciated. He was also avoided because he carried malaria parasites in his blood stream. Many who came very close to him got infected with malaria. Most animals therefore kept away from him.

The mosquito never paid heed to what was said about him, accusing the others of being jealous of him because he was an active young insect.

He prided himself in having the best singing voice in the whole wide jungle. The mosquito was a noisy character, with an annoying habit of disturbing meetings of the animals. The other animals saw him as rather verbose and ponderous, with intellectual pretensions, while he saw himself as a gifted poet and singer.

To avoid the nuisance from the mosquito, the animals often held their meetings by the seaside where there was usually a great amount of wind. Whenever the pesky mosquito stood up to contribute to the proceedings, the wind would simply sweep him off his perch and would carry him far away from the meeting place. By the time he would come back, the meeting would be over.

One hot afternoon while he was dozing under a green leaf, he overheard the big elephant discussing with another animal. The other animal wanted to know if the mighty elephant had parents. Considering his great size, the curious mosquito wondered how mighty his parents must be.

The wise elephant explained to the inquisitive insect that size did not determine one's age, and that if the mosquito were married, he too would have children. The other animals laughed uproariously, imagining the tiny mosquito having children. The animals wondered aloud if mosquito's children would be big enough for ordinary eyes to see them. But the mosquito did not find the joke funny so he made up his mind to put them to shame by marrying the prettiest lady in the land. He was determined to show those disrespectful animals that big brains and personalities were not necessarily to be found in big bodies.

Human beings were the leaders and most intelligent of all living things in those days, as they are still today. The mosquito felt a marriage relationship with human beings would attract a lot of respect towards him. He felt that the animals would begin to see him in a new light if he became an in-law to the most powerful creatures on earth.

He began therefore to woo different parts of the human body. He went to the nose first, but the nose said she was not interested. He next went to the eyes, which told him they did not believe in marriage, and before the mosquito could say any other word, the eyes fell asleep. The mosquito felt that the ease with which the eyes fell asleep made them incompatible, wondering if they would ever be awake long enough to perform their wifely duties.

So the mosquito went to the ears. Now the ears were the proudest of all the parts of the human body. They liked to bedeck themselves with earrings and jewelleries, especially during ceremonies. The ears considered themselves very pretty, and were generally considered to be egoistical. They had their own ideas about how their Mr Right would look like.

The marriage between the tongue and the thirty-two members of the teeth family was very much celebrated, and the envy of many. The tongue and her thirty-two husbands still live happily in the mouth to this day. The ears had always hoped that their own marriage would be as grand as that of the tongue, if not grander.

The ears felt extremely insulted when the mosquito came with his marriage proposal. They called him all sorts of names, including dead *insect talking*.

The right ear said that the way mosquito looked, he would most likely be dead by the following week. The left ear, which was known to be the saucier of the two sisters, spat at him and said she would be surprised if the emaciated and ill-looking mosquito lived to see the following day. The sisters pushed the mosquito out of their house and urged him to go and die in his own house. "We will come to your funeral tomorrow morning," they laughed at the poor unhappy mosquito.

The mosquito left, a humiliated man. But he was determined to have revenge because he felt the ears went too far. So every night, he would come and buzz noisily around their ears, reminding them that he was still alive, and powerful enough to prevent them from sleeping and also powerful enough to make them ill.

8

Why bats fly at night

The bat was seen as a bird as he was always with the birds. He was a very active bird, which tried hard to participate in the activities and meetings of the birds. The problem was that the birds never regarded him as a bird because his wife did not lay eggs like the other birds. Also, unlike the other birds, he did not have feathers. He had a black leathery skin. But he had wings like the other birds and therefore flew like a bird.

Whenever the birds were having a meeting and the bat came in, they would all stop talking until he had left. Behind his back, they gossiped that he did not have a beautiful face with a beak like them. They said he had the ugly face of a land animal, which to them, was enough to disqualify him from being a bird. They also ridiculed his skin for being too ugly and not feathery like theirs.

The discrimination and ill treatment from the birds made the bat choose to get closer to the land animals. He began therefore to attend the meetings of the land animals. Unfortunately for him again, the land animals were suspicious of him and did not fully welcome him to their gatherings. The animals regarded him as a bird. They said he had wings like a bird, and flew like a bird. They however never asked

him to leave their meetings but would not discuss any
important thing when he was in their midst.

The bat felt naturally upset and lonely.
One day he decided to do something about his
situation. He waited until the eagle, the king of the
birds, had gone out to find food for his nestlings and
went and took the young birds and killed them all.
He quickly plucked out their feathers and went and
put them in the lair of the king of the land animals.

When the kingbird came home and did not see his
babies, he raised an alarm, and all the birds came
around to help their king look for the missing
nestlings. They searched from tree to tree, in the tree
holes, on branches and leaves, but could not find
them. Then along came the bat. He told the birds he
knew were the little birds were. He then took them to
the den of the lion, were the birds saw the bones and
feathers of the dead little eaglets. The birds were very
upset. Immediately the birds declared war on the
land animals. The animals were equal to the situation.
The war started, and raged on for days.

The animals ate the roots of trees where the birds
made their nests and the trees fell down such that the
birds did not have anywhere to perch or make their
nests. The birds on the other hand pecked and clawed
on the animals from the air. Both the animals and the
birds lost a lot of their members in the fierce battle
that raged for days.

Meanwhile, the birds resolved to start welcoming
the bat to their meetings because of the role he played
in finding the killer of the eaglets. He was allowed to
the meetings where the birds planned their battle
strategies. Because of the war situation, the bat was
no longer discriminated against. The birds had

resolved that any animal that had wings and could fly must be regarded as a sibling.

After learning details of their war plans, the bat would sneak to a meeting of the land animals and reveal all he had heard. The land animals were very impressed and grateful, they resolved that the bat was a land animal, because like them, he neither had a beak, laid eggs nor had feathers. They began to allow him to attend their war cabinet meetings where they mapped out their strategies for the war. After learning of their war plans, the bat would reveal them to the birds. He felt he was taking his revenge for the way both the birds and the land animals had mistreated him over the years.

One day however the old vulture was outside the large compound where the animals were having an emergency meeting about the on-going war. The vulture was feasting on the carcasses of some dead animals when suddenly he looked into the compound and saw the bat mingling comfortably with the birds at the meeting. He strained his ears and looked closer and saw some of the war leaders giving the bat a bear hug and taking him aside to discuss with him in low tones.

The vulture immediately flew up onto a nearby tree and from there began shouting to the land animals that the bat was a traitor. He informed them that the bat was spying on them and was revealing their war plans to the birds. They blamed the bat's espionage activities for the unnecessary prolongation of the bloody war.

They planned to capture the bat but before they could seize him he quickly flew away. The land animals declared the bat wanted - dead or alive, and also informed the birds that he had been spying on them. The birds were very furious and also declared the bat an enemy, which must be captured dead or alive.

The bat knew he had become declared wanted dead or alive by both the land animals and the birds. He therefore decided to fly only at nights –when both the land animals and the birds would be comfortably asleep.

9

Why babies do not have teeth

Babies used to have teeth from birth. Their teeth were strong like those of adults. They could eat any kind of food - meat, fish, stockfish, hard nuts like palm nuts, coconuts, and other kinds of fruits.

The king of the land had a special hand stick. The stick was the king's symbol of authority. Whenever he held the stick, any pronouncement he made had the force of law, and was respected as such. No other person in the land had the right to hold that stick except the king.

The king had many enemies in the land so he protected his stick of authority jealously. The authority bestowed by this stick was based on its uniqueness. It had very strange carvings on it. These carvings were believed to have been made by the gods as the stick was presumed to have been given to the king by them.

One day, the queen gave birth to a baby boy. The king was overjoyed, as he had been wishing for a boy who would be the heir to the throne. The king made it a point of duty to see his little prince as often as he could. He usually saw him first thing in the morning and before he retired to bed in the night.

One day when the king went visiting his son in his princely chamber, he forgot his stick of authority in the baby's cot. Babies in those days, as today, liked putting whatever they could lay their hands on into their mouths; so by the time the king came back to retrieve his stick, the little prince had started chewing on it. He had used his strong teeth to remove all the strange carvings on the stick. Once those mystical carvings were chewed out of the stick, it became an ordinary stick, incapable of bestowing any authority to the king's pronouncements.

The king did not know what to do. The news spread fast all over the land that the king had lost his power because his stick of authority from the gods had been destroyed. His enemies were happy. They ridiculed him, and did every thing they could to humiliate and embarrass him.

The king was absolutely dismayed. He did not know whom to blame for his troubles. He could not blame the innocent baby. In his desperation, he began blaming everyone, including the gods, for creating little innocent children with teeth, which they used in destroying things, as they did not know the value of the things around them.

This of course upset the gods of the land and at the same time made them feel guilty for the king's woes. They decided therefore to remove the teeth of little babies. This they did by rubbing certain leaves on their gums and from that time babies were no longer born with teeth

10

Why we have rainfalls everywhere

King thunder used to be a great white ram. He was a magnificent-looking animal, with great curved horns and a long white beard. He also had a beautiful flowing mane.

His eyes emitted fire, which some people called lightening. His roars and belching came down as thunder.

King thunder was reputed to be a very short-tempered and violent king. Stories had it that he often came down on lonely and quiet spots in the farmlands to rest after his activities in the sky.

Normally, before coming down to the earth, he would inform all the other inhabitants of the sky not to disturb him while he was in his Camp Restplace, as he called it.

In those days, mother rain never rained at random and everywhere as she does these days. Rains used to fall only in exclusive places. For instance, if the owner of a particular farmland wished the rain to fall on his farmland, he would make certain sacrifices to mother rain and would beseech her to send rainfall to his farm. If she obliged, the rainfall would be limited to that farm only. If other farmers wanted rainfall, they too would make the request with the necessary sacrifices.

One day, king thunder came down to rest in a remote farmland in which the owner had made sacrifices to mother rain for her to fall upon it. Not aware of king thunder's presence in this farm, the rain fell upon it and subsequently beat king thunder and soaked him to the bone.

Thunder was very angry. In his rage, he flew back to the sky and berated the rain for beating him. He called her all sorts of insulting names. The poor, emotional lady rain was grossly upset. She wept bitterly and decided not to fall again. She became moody and withdrawn.

For months and years, the rain did not fall. The farmlands dried up, and so did the rivers, springs, streams and ponds. The people of the world started suffering. They called on mother rain to take pity on them. They made sacrifices and implored her not to let them all die of starvation.

Eventually the inhabitants of the sky took pity on the suffering people of the world and decided to call a meeting to discuss the issue.

Now the rain had many brothers and sisters, including snow who lived in the cold lands, her little sister, dew, who only came out in the mornings, and fog, who was forever moody and dour-faced. The rain also had many good friends such as the winds, who were always hyperactive. There were also the hurricane and the tornado, known for being on the violent side.

On the day of the meeting, rain's friends, siblings and relatives rallied around her against king thunder, which had few supporters – though it must be said he was very capable of taking care of himself. During the meeting, there was a heated exchange between the supporters of rain and thunder. King thunder was very infuriated and walked out, with threats to the rain.

Because of the threat to the life of madam rain, the winds volunteered to be her bodyguard and carried her wherever they went. They became her carriers. Therefore wherever they carried her to, she would fall there - sometimes in the sea, sometimes on farmlands, or cities, mountains or even in lonely places. And most of the time as she fell, one would hear king thunder still threatening her.

11

Why men no longer get pregnant

Men used to get pregnant and give birth like women do these days. It used to be that both the man and the woman could share the burden of the pregnancy. In those days, whenever the woman got tired of carrying the pregnancy, the man would take over.

The man and the woman lived happily, and loved each other very much. But every day, after the man had gone to the farm to work, the viper, a wicked snake that lived in a big tree nearby would come to the woman to taunt her. He would tell her that while she carried her pregnancy, the man was busy enjoying himself. The woman did not believe him, but she was pleased with the snake's companionship everyday. Each day she looked forward to seeing the snake when her husband had gone to the farm. The snake continued telling the woman lies about her husband. After a while the woman started believing the snake.

Unfortunately one day when the man came back from a meeting, he was drunk with palm wine. He was staggering all over the place and his speech was incoherent. When the woman saw her husband in that state, she was very disappointed, and that made her to fully believe all that the snake had been telling her about her husband.

The woman did not say any thing about the incident that day. She kept quiet until the following day when her husband was about to go out. She told him that she was ill and couldn't carry the pregnancy for that day. The husband therefore took the pregnancy over from her and carried it that day.

The following day, he asked his wife to take over the pregnancy, as he had to go to work. But the woman refused, saying that she was going to a distant farm to harvest yam that day. The following day again when he asked her to take over the pregnancy, she told him she had to go to the river to wash clothes, and therefore couldn't take the pregnancy from him. This continued for more than four months until it was almost time for the baby to be born.

The husband got very angry and insisted that it was time for his wife to take turn in carrying the pregnancy, that he had become tired of her excuses. But the wife became obstinate and refused to take over the pregnancy. There was a great quarrel between the woman and the man. The man therefore decided to report the case to the creator.

The great creator of all things was not happy about the problem between the man and his wife, because it was the man and the woman that he made the king and queen of all things that he created.

The creator decided to call a meeting of all creatures, with their wives.

The golden sun came with his silvery wife, the lunar queen, the moon.

The great mountain came with his mysterious wife, the valley.

The earth came with his expansive and extremely wide and lofty wife, the sky.

The land came with his sometimes peaceful and sometimes stormy wife, the sea.

The day came with his dark and ominous wife, the night.

The hot dry season also came with his wet, messy but luxuriant wife, the rainy season.

When they had all gathered and sat down, the creator explained why he had summoned the meeting. He told them that their king, the man, was having a dispute with his wife about who should carry the pregnancy for their forthcoming baby. He wanted to hear their opinions on the issue.

Immediately all the women in the meeting rose up and declared that it was their unanimous opinion that the man should carry the pregnancy as he was the stronger partner, instead of leaving his weak wife to carry such a heavy load alone for nine months while he went about drinking palm wine with his friends.

The men at the meeting also rose with one voice and insisted that the man was too busy to go about carrying such a heavy and delicate load while at the same time working hard on the farm. The males insisted that pregnancies were too fragile and delicate for the rough and hard man whose job was also rough and hard.

The women disagreed. Therefore there was a heated argument, which later degenerated into a messy brawl between the men and the women. The husbands separated from their wives. Accusations of being inconsiderate filled the air. The sky, which was at that time living with her husband, the earth, divorced her husband immediately and went to live up above, leaving the earth on his own. The valley divorced the mountain, her husband, and the sea also separated from her husband, the land, to live on her own. So did the sun and the moon, the night and the day, the rainy season and the dry season. All the wives went their ways and left their husbands on their own. But man refused to leave his wife and chose instead to make peace with her.

The others felt betrayed, and did not forgive man for this. They felt the fight had started in the first place because they wanted to defend their fellow male, the man. But then the man they were fighting for made up with his wife while they all divorced their own wives.

They held an emergency meeting about man's treachery and resolved never to have anything to do with him again. They also agreed that they would punish him and his offspring whenever they could. This explains why the sun beats him, the rain falls on him and every other element of nature torments him and his family.

This made the great creator very sad. To compensate the man for his loyalty, he took a decision that from thence only the woman would carry the pregnancy – from conception until the child was born. He also sought to mollify the woman by making the man responsible for protecting her and providing for her. The man was therefore forced to cut down the time he spent on enjoyment and palm wine drinking because he had to work extra hard to provide for the woman and her children.

The creator also decided to punish the snake that poisoned the woman's mind and started that misunderstanding between man and woman. He declared the snake man's mortal enemy and removed its legs and arms so that man could easily identify it.

How the frog got its big eyes

The frog was a very active member of the animal community. He was an amphibian. He lived both in the water and on the land. He knew the secrets of the waters and also all that happened on the land. If the land animals had messages for their friends in the water, it was usually the frog that they sent to deliver such a message. And if those in the water had something for those on the land, it was the frog that was also sent on such errands.

One day, the golden ring of the king of the animals got missing. All the animals denied knowledge of the whereabouts of the ring. All the wise animals tried to find out who stole the ring but without any success. The animals therefore decided to consult the oracle. The oracle advised them to consult the wise ones in the water.

The king then sent for the frog, and told him what the oracle had said about his missing ring.

The frog left for the seabed. He returned to the king after several days to say that the wise ones of the deep blue sea, after their incantations, concluded that an animal with a hard shell had swallowed the ring.

The tortoise was summoned to the presence of the king since he was the only animal known to have a hard shell. Of course he vehemently denied the allegation. Instead he accused the frog of not going into the seabed to consult the wise ones as demanded by the king but just wanted to use him as a scapegoat to cover up his negligence of duty. He claimed the frog never liked him and had some personal scores to settle with him.

The animals did no believe the tortoise. In a meeting summoned by the king, it was agreed that the frog should follow the tortoise wherever he went, even when he went to the toilet – to see if he would pass out the ring in his stool.

The tortoise agreed to this arrangement. He pretended not to be worried at all. As soon as the animals dispersed from the meeting, the tortoise too got up to leave. But the frog tried to deter him: "Where do you think you are going?" he asked, grabbing his arms to prevent him from leaving.

The tortoise got all excited. "Ah ah, you are asked to keep an eye on me, not to hold me with your hands."

The tortoise then took some alligator pepper from his bag and started chewing it. He told the frog: "Better look at me hard. You see, I am a magician, and if you do not look at me closely enough, with your eyes widely open, I may disappear."

The frog therefore looked at the tortoise closely with his eyes widely open. The tortoise instantly spat the spate of the hot and painful alligator pepper into the frog's eyes. The poor frog screamed with pain, rubbing desperately his itching eyes with his hands. The pepper hurt him more, so he rubbed his eyes with sand but the pain did not go away. He got leaves - both dried and wet ones, and put them over his eyes but these too did not help.

All the animals came and helped. Some rubbed the frog's eyes with salt, and some tried fresh palm oil, and some, three-day old palm wine but nothing provided any succour to the frog who was writhing in pains. Every one present tried something. By the time the wise old elephant came around and advised them to use water, the frog's eyes had swollen very much. That is why to this day, the frog has big eyes.

13

How the nightingale got a melodious voice

The nightingale used to be just an ordinary bird with a dull plumage. It had a little body, and its voice was terrible and harsh. When the nightingale spoke, the sound grated on the ears and those present would always hush him down. When the birds went for important outings or meetings, the nightingale was strictly warned not to speak in order not to embarrass them with his coarse voice.

Despite his voice, the nightingale was an agile little bird. Ever busy and active, he was quite sharp, ever ready to help folks, and extremely diligent too. Though he has a bad voice, friends and families loved having the lithe little bird around.

The nightingale was not happy, especially at nights. Every night he continued to practice various songs, hoping that his voice would get better. But the more he practiced and trained his voice, the worse it got.

One night while the nightingale was trying his best to sing a song, he saw a strange little bird pass by. The bird was limping from tree to tree. It seemed to be in terrible pain. Immediately the ever-caring nightingale ran to the bird's aid and inquired o f the bird what its problem was, but the sick bird did not speak a word. The nightingale thought this odd, but all the same he went on and prepared a portion of herbs and roots, which he made the sick little bird to drink. The strange bird drank it all, and after a short while, it spread its wing and flew around a bit, then it flew about in wider and wider circles. It returned to where the nightingale was waiting and spoke for the first time. It told the helpful nightingale that it was a spirit bird, on an errand from the spirit land to a distant place. The strange bird said it had been attacked by some night birds on its way back but had managed to escape.

The nightingale observed that the strange bird had a very melodious voice. Therefore when the grateful spirit bird asked the nightingale what it could do for him in return for his kindness, the nightingale narrated the problems he had been having because of his bad voice.

The spirit bird then plucked out one of its feathers and put it in its mouth. After a while, it brought it out, made certain incantations and then put the feather into the nightingale's mouth. Then the strange spirit bird flew away into the night from whence it had come. The nightingale immediately fell asleep.

He woke up very ill the following morning. He took some of the herb and root portion he had earlier given to the strange spirit bird. By night, when he tried to sing, his throat was sore. However to his surprise, with more attempts, better sound started coming out. Soon the voice got much better, stronger and acquired a melodious quality.

The following morning the bird community woke up to the sound of a spiritual music, such that they had never heard before. They were all surprised and quickly gathered to find out who had such a melodious voice. And behold it was the nightingale! The nightingale has retained that beautiful voice to this day.

14

How the dog came to live with man

In the olden days, dogs lived in the great jungle with other beasts of the forest.

One day the animals decided to build a big house where they could all stay during thunderstorms. They also agreed that the house would be used for their meetings and festivals.

The building commenced. The elephant and the buffalo used their great strength to drag big timber and logs to the building site. The smaller animals fetched and carried whatever they could. Some brought sand, some brought wood, some, raffia and others, palm fronds. The birds brought vines and ropes from creeper plants.

The monkeys worked very hard, placing the logs on top of each other and doing most of the carpentry work. The dog and the lion supervised the project. Soon the house began to take shape and was eventually completed.

When it was completed, it turned out to be a great and beautiful house, with a mighty hall for meetings and other smaller rooms for tired animals to rest in. The butterflies were asked to paint the house. This, they happily and willingly did. The great animal house in the jungle was an exceptionally beautiful house.

Every animal loved the house, especially the lion. So one day the lion said to himself: "I am the strongest animal in the jungle. Why do I have to share the same house with all these weak animals?" So he gathered his belongings and moved into the house.

If any other animal came near to that house, the lion would roar and frighten the animal away. The animals were all afraid of the lion because of his great strength and dangerous claws and fangs.

The other animals did not know what to do. They therefore decided to wait for the dog, which was away on a long journey to come back. The dog came back that day, and immediately all the animals trooped to his house. The dog was taken aback, and addressed them thus: "My fellow animals, what is the reason for this gathering in front of my house, and why are you all wearing sad expressions?"

The elephant said "The goat has eaten palm frond on my head."

The tiger answered: "We have washed our hands and cracked palm kernel for the chicken." The less tactful antelope said, "We have built a house for another to live in."

The dog was confused.

"What are you all talking about? Will someone please explain to me what is going on here? Has our great house fallen? And where is the lion?"

The elephant then stepped forward and told the dog all that had happened. The dog became terribly upset. He immediately set off to the big animal house to confront the lion about what he heard.

He got there and met the lion, which growled and roared menacingly. The dog was not afraid. He entered into the house and demanded an explanation from the lion why he thought he had the right to move into a house built by all the animals. The lion was angered at the dog's audacity and lack of respect and asked him to leave immediately. The dog ignored the order and threat from the lion and instead began throwing the lion's property out of the house.

A fight immediately broke out between the two.

They fought long and hard inside the house. Sometimes, the animals would hear the dog barking furiously, and they would cheer in jubilation. At other times they would hear the lion roaring and they would tremble with fear. The two animals fought from morning till noon, into the night, until the following morning.

They continued the fight the following morning even though they were both tired. At last the dog made one mighty effort and bit the lion on the ear, very hard. The pain was too much and the lion ran out of the house into the forest. The animals cheered happily. They all rushed into the house and carried the dog shoulder high.

After a long time however, when the dog had once again gone on one of his long journeys, the crafty lion returned and summoned all the animals to a meeting. He served them a lot of food and strong palm wine. Many of the animals drank rather too much and were drunk. When the lion saw that many of the animals were drunk, he told them that the dog had chased him out of the house only because he was planning to move in there alone. He also told them that the dog had perfected plans to seize the house as soon as he returned.

Because the animals were very drunk and therefore unable to reason properly, they believed everything the lion told them. They asked the lion what they should do. The scheming lion, then told them to lie in wait for the dog and ambush him on his return.

The drunken animals agreed and waited for the dog by the bush path leading to his house. They attacked him as he was coming home. The dog was very surprised, and ran away from the forest where he lived. He could not understand why the animals he had sacrificed his life for would now attack him. He began to run, believing that the best thing to do was to run away from the danger first and then think properly on how to respond to the attack.

He continued to run until he came to the land of man. The man welcomed him, listened very sympathetically to his story and advised him that revenge was a dish that was best served cold. The dog never forgot this advice just as he never forgot the attack from the other animals. He swore he must have his revenge, and that he must have it *as a cold dish*. Therefore he decided to live with his new friend, the man, to have all the time he needed to plan his revenge.

B
Moral stories

15

The tortoise tries to dodge his responsibilities

Once upon a time, the tortoise observed with increasing apprehension the failing health of his old mother. It became quite obvious to him with each passing day that she was not likely to recover from her sickness. The sly tortoise examined his finances and felt there was no way he could afford the burial rites of his mother.

The custom of the people forbade using poverty as an excuse to avoid giving one's departed parents a befitting funeral. In fact, it had never been heard of that anyone tried to evade that responsibility on any ground. The person was sure to be made the laughing stock of the entire village. The irony however was that it was almost impossible to borrow money from any one to fulfil that obligation. Who would have the heart to ask a bereaved one to pay back a loan?

So the sneaky tortoise decided to do what he was best at - dodging his responsibilities. The following morning therefore he announced to all the animals in his village that he was embarking on a very long journey to a distant land. He asked them not to bother to come looking for him, especially if something natural, and which had always happened in their village, happened again while he was away on his long journey. If on the other hand, something unnatural, something unimaginable, something that had never happened before in their land happened while he was away, then they had his permission to come and look for him.

Not long after the tortoise left, his poor, old and sick mother died.

"Ohooo," said the villagers. "Is this why that crafty tortoise told us not to come looking for him if something that had been happening in the village happened again, knowing quite well that death is not a novelty here?" The villagers were upset with such a shameless display of irresponsibility by one of their own. They began therefore to plan how to get the sly tortoise to come home and face his responsibilities. They thought and thought. Then the old, wise elephant hit on a brilliant idea. He quickly summoned a meeting and revealed his plan to the other animals. They all agreed to the plan.

The next day, the fastest of the animals, the cheetah, the monkey, the antelope and the hare were dispatched to the four cardinal points in the village - one to the east, one to the west, the other two to the northern and southern directions respectively. They were to go and find the tortoise and bring him back home, fast.

It was the hare that eventually caught up with him.

"Ho ho, brother tortoise," he hailed.

The tortoise, hearing his name mentioned, thought his fellow villagers had come looking for him, and immediately tried to dodge into some thicket. When he realised he had been seen, he winced, anticipating to be told his mother had died.

"Ah! brother hare, what brings you so far from home?", he asked in pretended surprise.

74

"It's you I am looking for," said the hare.

"Oh, why? I thought I told you folks at home that it has to take an abnormal occurrence for you to come searching for me. You know I am…"

"Ahhh brother tortoise," the wily hare interrupted him. "The entire land has turned upside down. The things that are happening in our land have never happened before, and I pray they never will happen again. My eyes have beheld my ears. Our poor land has become contaminated. I tell you brother tortoise, it is sacrilegious."

The hare continued. "I wish I had died last year, or as a child. In fact, I wish I had not been born to…."

"What happened?", asked the tortoise, curious.

"Oh oh oh if I had not beheld these frightening occurrences with my two naked eyes I could not have believed them," he said and shook his head sadly. "Oh, how can I narrate such a terrible story to my grand children and admit that it happened in my time and in this our land."

"What happened my friend? Tell me what happened and quit rambling." The tortoise was both anxious and worried.

The dramatic hare then went into the next stage of his acting. He broke down and started weeping. "Oh, we have lost our dear land, can we ever purify it after these weird occurrences. Can the animals of the land hold their heads high after this – this…?" Words failed him. Tears cascaded down his face.

The tortoise was visibly shaken. He grabbed the sobbing hare by the shoulder and shook him wildly.

"Will you tell me what happened in our land, you stupid animal. Did you come all this way to show me how to cry? Come on, out with it."

The hare controlled himself. He wiped his face, and sat down on a fallen tree trunk. "Do you have a little snuff on you?" he asked.

The tortoise promptly produced his snuffbox and handed it over.

"Thanks." He went through the ritual of snuffing, slowly and deliberately.

"Sit down," he advised the tortoise, patting the tree trunk he was sitting on. "You may fall down when I tell you the eerie tales that I bear."

The anxious tortoise sat next to the hare.

"We woke up two days ago, and lo and behold all the dogs in the land had grown horns."

"Whaaaaat! " screamed the tortoise.

"By the afternoon of the same day, male animals were getting pregnant," the hare continued in a most solemn tone.

"Unbelievable!" shouted the tortoise.

The hare continued. "By next morning, what did we behold, but trees bearing wrong fruits. Palm trees were bearing coconut fruits; corn stalks became heavy with tomatoes and pepper, pears. You remember that my sweet pear tree? It was bearing guava, for goodness sake, guava fruits."

As he spoke, the tortoise was only thinking of returning to his village to see these developments for himself.

But the crafty hare was not done yet.

"By afternoon the next day, some reptiles began to fly. There has been pandemonium in the land I tell you, it is...'

The tortoise did not wait for the hare to complete the last sentence before he began running back home – as fast as he could. He had always believed he was a very important figure in the community and could not imagine himself not being around when such great events were happening in his village. He believed that without his presence, it might be difficult to find someone in the village that could re-tell and interpret the unfolding stories as perfectly as they should be. He increased his pace. The more he thought about it the faster he ran. He did not even wait for the hare.

When he got to his village, tired but excited, he was promptly grabbed by the other animals and taken to where the corpse of his old mother was lying in state.

"A man cannot run away from his shadow," they told him.

"This is your responsibility, you have to face it," the gathered villagers said in unison, pointing to tortoise's dead mother.

16

The Race

The antelope is a beautiful animal, with a beautiful, colourful skin and branched horns. He is fleet-footed and elegant but unfortunately a very selfish and proud animal. He looks down on all the other animals that are less elegant than himself. He particularly liked to pick on little animals like the tortoise. He got some sadistic pleasures from undermining and ridiculing such animals. Most of his victims did not care about him but the tortoise felt deeply hurt by the antelope's constant meanness.

One day while the animals were on a community work programme, the antelope shouted at the tortoise to get out of the way, and let more worthy animals (like himself) pass. The pompous antelope did not stop there. He further told the tortoise that he and his entire kindreds were slow coaches, both physically and mentally. Some of the animals present objected strongly to that insult by the antelope.

"No, no, Mister antelope, that is taking it a little too far. I mean to call his entire family slow coaches is not fair at all," the monkey objected.

The antelope retorted, "Oh oh, are you implying that they are not slow coaches? Then let them run, and let us see how fast they are." He laughed at his own silly joke.

The hippopotamus pointed out to the antelope, that running was not the only asset an animal needed in order to survive in the jungle.

The tortoise, who was obviously hurt by the antelope's caustic remarks, surprised every animal there by throwing a challenge: "If the antelope wants a race, I am ready to give him one," he said. There was a hush among the animals. One of them guffawed unconsciously and then burst out laughing. Soon there was a hearty and uproarious laughter among all the animals. The antelope laughed the loudest. The tortoise did not join in the laughter. He waited patiently until they had all stopped laughing, then he repeated what he had said earlier, very calmly: "I am willing and ready to give the big headed antelope a racing competition." Again the animals dabbled into a rib-cracking laughter. The tortoise then repeated the challenge for a third time.

This time the elephant stepped forward and asked the tortoise if he was serious about such a challenge. The tortoise used the opportunity to address the animals: "You are all aware of the way the antelope has been deriving sadistic pleasure from ridiculing me, especially in the public. Now he has extended it to my entire family. Well, our people say that it is only a tree that stands still when it is threatened; a real animal has to fight back, especially in a situation like this, in order to defend his family's honour. I am very serious about the challenge. I demand that necessary arrangements be made to hold this race."

The elephant, which was the patron of the animals, turned to the antelope to know his position on the issue. The antelope said he found the whole challenge ridiculous and that he had no intentions of being a party to such idiocy.

The elephant had to painstakingly explain to the not- so-bright antelope the implications of backing down from such a challenge. It would mean, he said, that he (the antelope) did so out of fear of humiliation. And their custom demanded that in such a situation, he would have to curtsy to the tortoise whenever their paths crossed. Backing out, the antelope was told, would also mean, as their custom again demanded, that whenever the tortoise sent him on an errand, no matter how lowly, he would be bound to obey. Also, backing out would mean that whenever the animals gather for a meeting or festival, the antelope must never speak before the tortoise and he must never contradict or disagree with any statement made by Mr tortoise. Hearing these, the antelope spat into the bush in disgust, *tufiakwa*! "May the ancestors forbid, that 1, Honourable Mr antelope, should be so humbled and subordinated to the dull and dumb tortoise," he said.

He accepted the challenge.

Three animals, the dog, the monkey and the leopard were asked to take charge of arranging the competition. The tortoise was asked to choose the route where the race would be run. He chose a village, three days journey from theirs. The antelope not knowing why the tortoise chose that particular route, agreed. The panel then fixed the date for the race, four market days from the time the challenge was thrown and accepted.

The panel suggested that two pairs of batons be carved. One set in black, which should be collected by both the tortoise and the antelope at the starting point of the race and the other set, in white, to be received by them at the other end. Each contestant would hand in the black baton at the other end of the race and would receive a white baton in return. Whoever submitted his white baton to the leopard at the finishing line of the race would be declared the winner.

The dog was to take off immediately with the set of white batons, to wait at the other end. The monkey was to monitor the race from a tree branch while the leopard was to be at the starting point, which was also the race's finishing line. He would also receive the set of white batons to determine the winner.

That evening, the tortoise called the whole tortoise colony, and explained to them what was going on. He reminded them of how the antelope had always insulted their tribe in public, and how the antelope had addressed them collectively as slow coaches. Well he, Mr tortoise had challenged their tormentor to a racing competition to enable him wipe out such an insulting label.

The entire tortoise tribe agreed to encourage him in whatever way they could. They agreed there was a need to teach the stupid antelope a lesson. The tortoise confided his strategy to his tribal members and explained to them, that the route he chose for the race, was part of that strategy. The route led to a fast - flowing river, with the only bridge being a narrow-stemmed palm tree that fell across the river. The tortoise had calculated that the wide-footed antelope could not easily cross through this narrow bridge when he reached the river.

The tortoise also told the other tortoises that they had to race through a dense forest, with very low and thick foliage. He again explained that his strategy was that the big-horned antelope would have problems untangling his horns from the intertwining low branches, creepers, vines and leaves of the forest. He told them that he expected to take advantage of the inevitable delays the antelope would suffer. The tortoise assured his kindred that he could easily cross the narrow bridge and creep through the undergrowth of the thick forest without problems.

The tortoise also told them that the route passed through a field with a lot of succulent grass, which the antelope would find too tempting to resist. He assured them that once the antelope had fed fat on the succulent grass, he would want to have a nap. He also told them that there were a lot of other animals on that field that were from the same kingdom as the antelope such as the eland, elk and zebra. He explained that his other strategy was that the antelope would not be able to resist the temptation to play with his kind before continuing with the race, which again would delay him.

The other tortoises agreed to place themselves at strategic points along the race route, and to try as much as they could to distract or even totally discourage the antelope from the race. They were sure that the antelope would not be able to recognise one tortoise from the other.

On the appointed day before cockcrow, the two competitors arrived at the village square, which was the starting point of the race. There, they met the leopard and the monkey. The leopard gave each a black baton. At the first cockcrow, the leopard struck the gong and the race began. Both contestants took off with great speed and determination, the antelope leaping, while the tortoise crawled as fast as he could.

The antelope arrived at the fast-flowing river first. He stood for sometime, trying to figure out how to cross the river. In desperation, he tried to swim across but all his efforts proved to be in vain. He was still trying to figure out how to cross the river when the tortoise arrived there and crossed over with ease. After many attempts, the antelope eventually succeeded in crossing over.

As the tortoise saw him coming, he hid under a shrub, and the antelope ran past him. The antelope increased his speed, trying to catch up and overtake the tortoise. But ran as he did, he could not see the tortoise. He was surprised and began to wonder whether the tortoise had run so far ahead of him in so short a time.

Suddenly, the antelope looked at a corner. And there was the tortoise relaxing under the shade of a tree, nonchalantly. The antelope was rather surprised at the very relaxed mood he saw the tortoise in.

"Hey Mister antelope, where are you hurrying to?" the tortoise called.

"Ah ah," replied the antelope. "What about our race, are you not continuing with it?"

"Oh, that race? You mean you really took that joke serious. What makes you think I can seriously challenge a fleet- footed wonder like you to a race? Come on, my friend, that was a joke. Forget it, okay?"

"I could have thought so" the antelope said, not knowing that the tortoise he was talking to was not the same as the tortoise he was competing against, but his brother. The antelope then relaxed under a tree shade and soon dozed off. By the time he woke up, the tortoise had gone. The antelope assumed that the tortoise had gone home. So he turned back and started heading home.

The monkey who was monitoring the race from a treetop suddenly could no longer see the antelope.

Fearing that some mishap might have befallen him, he went in search of him. He caught up with the antelope as he had just managed to cross that fast-flowing river, on his way home. On asking why he was returning home, the antelope told the monkey that the tortoise had called off the race.

"But where is the tortoise?" the monkey asked. It was then that the antelope remembered that he had not passed the tortoise on his way home. "Well, even if the tortoise has called off the race, the other animals have not called it off. So you still have to hand over the white baton to the leopard to be declared the winner," the monkey advised him.

The antelope took the advice and turned back. But again, he spent considerable time trying to cross the fast-flowing river. He eventually succeeded again but that was only after he had spent the night resting. The antelope therefore wasted one full day while the tortoise, which was running at his slow but steady pace, gained one day.

The antelope, realising now that he had lost one whole day, decided to run faster. Anyway, he told himself, even if the tortoise had a two-day start on him, he would still finish the race ahead of him. As the antelope ran as fast as he could, he suddenly came to the thick forest and his horns were unfortunately caught and tangled by some creepers and low vines. He spent another full day trying to untangle his horns. When he eventually managed to free himself, he felt very exhausted and hungry.

He did not have the strength to run any longer. He walked slowly and soon came to an open field where some animals of his ilk were playing. The antelope immediately joined them. He first of all ate to his heart's content, and then played gleefully with his mates. He felt very tired afterwards and decided to have some sleep. Another day passed.

At this point the antelope calculated that running through the river, the thick forest, the green field and the long stretch of road had taken him six days. This worried him greatly. He still needed to get to the dog and his white baton. He however consoled himself with the fact that it would take at least seven days for the slow tortoise to get to the dog. He started off again at a very fast pace.

As he turned the corner however, he saw the tortoise slowly heading in a different direction. The antelope knew the tortoise was taking the wrong direction but reasoned that it must be the taking of shortcuts that had made it possible for the very slow tortoise to keep pace with him. So he also took that direction, believing it to be a shortcut. The antelope again failed to discover that it was not the tortoise he was competing against that took that direction, but his cousin. The antelope ran for half the day but when he realised that he had not come to any recognisable landmark to indicate that he was on the right track, he turned back and began to retrace his steps. By the time he got to the right track, another day had been lost, and he still had a full day's journey to get to the dog and the white baton.

Suddenly he saw the tortoise coming back from the opposite direction with his own white baton. He then estimated that from where he was, it would take him two days to get to the dog and receive a white baton and another day to get back to the point where he was. The tortoise now had three clear days' advantage over him.

It took the antelope three days from where he was to reach the dog, collect his white baton and get to the thick forest. Once again, his horns got entangled in the forest and he had to use a lot of time and energy in untangling them. When eventually he succeeded in freeing the horns, he was tired and hungry. As he walked hungrily, he suddenly noticed a trail of salt on the track. The antelope loved salt, and being very hungry, decided to help himself on it.

By the time he had finished licking the salt, he was very thirsty. Luckily, there was a pot of fresh palm wine at the foot of a tree. He quickly guzzled it up. Then he started feeling dizzy and decided to lie down and rest a bit. Quickly, he fell asleep. By the time he woke up, it was night and so dark that he could not see clearly enough to travel through the dense forest. He therefore spent the night there.

Another day was lost.

He took off again very early in the morning. By this time the tortoise was way ahead of him. It took the antelope two more days of running and resting to get to the fast-flowing river. As he got to the river, he saw the tortoise crossing it. The antelope was happy. He had stretched himself to his limit and therefore decided to rest a bit before attempting to cross the treacherous river. He assured himself that even if it took him half the day to cross the river, he would surely overtake the tortoise and get to the leopard before him.

Shortly after crossing the river, he saw the tortoise crawling along sluggishly. He zoomed past him with a shout of joy.

At the next turning to the left however, he saw a lot of animals gathering. They were all excitedly watching something happening at the centre of the circle. The finishing point for the race was just about a hundred metres ahead. The curious antelope decided to find out what the object of attraction was. He reasoned that getting to the finishing line was a matter of only a few jumps and he would of course win the race.

In the centre of the circle were some tortoises holding a circus. They were all funnily dressed. The tortoises were attempting to build a pyramid, but were falling over themselves and laughing uproariously. The antelope was promptly caught in the excitement. Some animals were throwing rotten fruits and abuses at the tortoises, and of course the antelope joined them. He was so engrossed in abusing the tortoises that he did not notice his opponent, the tortoise crawl pass. By the time he recollected himself and decided to continue the race, the tortoise was very close to the finishing line. The antelope put on a desperate chase, hoping to pass him before he would hand over his white baton to the waiting leopard. He was just a foot behind as the tired tortoise handed over his baton to the leopard.

The tortoise had won the race. As he was declared the winner by the judges, the antelope was warned henceforth to stop molesting the tortoise and his people. When asked how he managed the astounding feat of beating the antelope in a race, the tortoise simply said: "Slow and steady wins a race." In his mind he thought: "Family is strength."

<u>17</u>

The tortoise and his bag of wisdom

The tortoise usually prided himself in being the wisest of all animals. He liked to show off his wisdom by either fabricating stories of adventures to distant and exotic lands or by telling tall tales of escapades with non-existent birds in non-existent valleys or caves. But most members of the animal kingdom were often impressed by his tales and regarded him as a hero.

Only the snail, which lived in a shell like the tortoise, knew that the tortoise was a great fibber.

One day, after the tortoise had stayed up late entertaining the animals with his lies and stories, he came back home with a big headache. He could not understand why he had such a terrible headache. He complained to his friend, the snail. The snail knew that the tortoise had not had a good sleep recently because he was always out late telling tall tales and talking too much. The snail knew that the combination of the two would be enough to give any one a headache.

The snail did not want to tell the tortoise that. Rather he challenged him: "I thought you knew everything, then why don't you know the reason for your headache?"

At this, the tortoise, which liked to be seen as an accomplished philosopher, who had answers to any type of question, began to think hard. "I think it is the envy of the other animals over my great wisdom that is causing the headache," he said.

The snail laughed. "No, I think it is actually the great knowledge you carry in your head that is giving you this headache. No one can have so much wisdom as you have without having some sort of headache now and again." The tortoise liked the answer, and promptly agreed with him despite the fact that the snail was only pulling his legs.

"That is true, my friend, very very true," the tortoise announced, nodding his head in total agreement to what his friend had just said.

The tortoise continued: "So what do we do about it, my friend. What is your suggestion? Now bear in mind that I know what to do, I only want to find out if you also know what to do in such situations," he added.

The snail, amused, decided to play along with him.

"Well, why don't you put the whole wisdom in your head into a big calabash and keep it in a safe place, so that when you need any particular wise thing, you can go there and retrieve it. After usage you can put it back into the calabash. In that way, you won't need to carry much wisdom in your head, and you will spare yourself from having headaches"

"That's a good idea, a very good idea," said the tortoise. "I will bring a very large gourd, and put my head into it until all my wisdom have transferred into it, then I will keep it on top of a very high tree, so that no other animal can get at it."

The tortoise went off to fetch a gourd. The snail asked some bees sucking nectar from nearby flowers to go and call all the other animals to come and witness the interesting show. Within a short time, all the animals gathered. They saw the tortoise with his head in a large calabash. The snail explained to them what was going on. The animals shook their heads in total disbelief at such apparent stupidity.

After a while, the tortoise brought out his head from the gourd and quickly covered the mouth of the gourd so that none of the wisdom he had apparently transferred into it would escape. He carried the gourd to the foot of a very tall tree and tried to climb the tree with the gourd on his head. This proved to be impossible, as he needed his two hands to hold the gourd on his head. The gathered animals, from where they hid themselves, began to laugh. The 'wise' tortoise then transferred the calabash to his stomach, and tried to climb the tree again, but again it was not possible as the calabash prevented him from having a firm grip of the tree.

The snail then suggested to the tortoise to place the calabash on his back and tie it with a string across his stomach. This he did and found out that he could easily climb the tree this way. As he started climbing the tree, the animals could no longer contain themselves and they burst into uproarious laughter. The tortoise, hearing the uproar became frightened, not knowing if the village had come under an attack. In that momentary distraction, he lost his hold and fell down heavily, breaking the large gourd containing his wisdom. Tears were flowing down the cheeks of the animals as they laughed heartily at the tortoise. The tortoise saw them laughing at him and was greatly embarrassed. The snail moved to him where he was writhing in pain and said gently, "You see my friend, pride goes before a big fall."

The incident greatly humbled the tortoise and he stopped laying claim to being the wisest animal in the land.

18

The lion and the mouse

Tami, the mouse, was rummaging through fallen leaves and scampering up and down little trees, foraging for his lunch. There were so many insects and nuts in the neighbourhood and Tami was having a good time stuffing himself.

In his excitement, he temporarily forgot his natural alertness and caution, which had saved him many times from many dangerous situations in the forest where he lived.

Tami was enjoying himself on a particularly stubborn insect when he sighted a well-nourished grasshopper. Grasshoppers had always been his favourite prey and he hadn't eaten any for weeks. He quickly spat out the insect he was struggling to eat and gave the grasshopper a chase. The grasshopper was swift, but Tami pursued her with nimbleness. As he pursued the grasshopper, he suddenly burst out through an undergrowth and *wham* into the paws of Zimba - the great lion, king of all the animals.

The wily little mouse realised with a great failing of the spirit that death was staring him in the face. He realised that he had to come up with something exceptionally clever otherwise he would become history.

He bowed his head in reverence to the lion.

"Oh king, oh mighty one. I was around the vicinity, and I noticed you were trying to have your well deserved rest, but these pesky little insects keep disturbing you, so I decided to drive them away so that my king can have a comfortable rest."

The lion nodded his head and smiled mischievously. "And you must know too that I am hungry and that you are going to be my lunch," he told the scared little mouse.

"Ha ha ha, oh majestic king, you have a great sense of humour. That is why you are our king. Who can think that you, in all your mightiness and royalty, will eat a puny, bony, undernourished, dirty, smelly runt like me? Ha ha ha, that is unthinkable."

That got to the lion. He blinked once, twice. "But I am hungry, and I've got to eat something," he insisted.

Tami immediately capitalised on the lion's momentary indecision to press his case.

"Yet, oh great king, but you have to eat something that befits a king, not a thing like me. And anyway, if you, oh king eat up all your loyal subjects like me, who then will you rule over, who will be your loyal subjects, who will you send on errands, who will drive away your enemies like those cheeky little insects?"

The lion nodded his royal head in total agreement. He was quite impressed by the witty, little rodent's efforts to save his life. He decided to exercise his power as the king and set him free.

"I am letting you go free, not because of your flippant lies, but because you little runt have some nerve." And he let the mouse out of his clutches. The tough little mouse bowed to the lion and said: "The power of a king is not to kill, for any wretched little beast can waste another life, but the main power is giving life, exercising mercy and granting pardon to people whom he easily could have killed. Only the king possesses that. I am grateful to you for your kindness today. Believe me, I will one day repay this debt."

The lion waved his great paw and Tami dived, and immediately disappeared into the undergrowth.

One evening, some weeks after Tami's encounter with Zimba, while the normal activities in the animal kingdom were going on, a mighty roar suddenly filled the air.

Every creature within the vicinity froze in its track. The insects and the birds quit chirping. The chewing, munching and rummaging by the animals all suddenly went rigid. Both predators and the preys all froze on their tracks, their senses though remained alert.

Suddenly there was another frightening roar. This broke the tension. This time all the animals took flight in different directions for safety. Every animal promptly found a hiding place and dived into it. They sensed that whatever was releasing those ear-piercing roars must surely be a threat to animal life.

Tami was munching a nut when he heard the first roar. At the second scream, he darted sharply into an underbrush, with all his senses alert. It was in this state of full alertness that Tami heard a noise that sounded like a groan or a moan, indicating that some one was in terrible pain.

There was a third thunderous roar, after which there was relative quiet. But Tami continued listening with apt concentration. Once again he heard the groaning of what seemed to be of an animal in excruciating pains. Tough little Tami decided to go and investigate. He started creeping cautiously towards the direction of the roars. As he got closer, the moans and groans became more audible. At last he came to a spot, and to his surprise, there was Zimba, the great lion, rolled over on his back, his legs waving frantically in the air. The sight left the little mouse confused. What was going on here?

Tami was bemused to see the king of the animals in this humbling position. It was obvious to him that it was the lion that had been roaring and moaning alternately all this while.

Eventually Tami decided to announce his presence. Perhaps, he could help in some ways, he thought. He coughed loud enough for the lion to hear. The lion summoned up courage and quickly stood up but was overwhelmed by the pain. He screamed, his face contorted in pain. "Who are you, what are you doing here?" he screamed at the mouse. "Come on, get out of here!"

But Tami was unimpressed. He knew that the big animal was in trouble.

"What is your trouble?" Tami asked sympathetically, but from a safe distance.

Zimba jerked around. "Are you still here you little pest, come on get lost."

"You are in pain, can I help?"

"And what do you think you can do?" Zimba asked, inadvertently conceding he was in trouble.

"Tell me first how you want me to help, then we will take it from there."

Zimba considered him for one moment. He stretched out on the ground, and raised his right front paw. It was all swollen and bloody. A great thorn was sticking out of it.

With the deftness with which the mouse had been reputed to steal, he swiftly removed the offending thorn from the lion's paw. The lion was greatly relieved and thanked the mouse profusely. "One for me, one for you," Tami said

"One good turn deserves another, eh?" Zimba said, smiling, impressed by the gallantry of the brave little mouse.

"Yes, live and let live," Tami concurred as he disappeared again into the under growth.

19

The tough Cockerel

It was a normal morning in the fowl community in the courtyard. Bunki, the cockerel, was strutting around proudly content and pleased with his ever-growing family of five hens and more than fifteen chickens.

The hens with their respective broods were scattered all over the courtyard, doing what they were best at doing - scratching, pecking, clucking and feeding.

The atmosphere in the courtyard was relaxed and serene. Suddenly, out of the darkening blue sky, the hawk struck. The serenity of the atmosphere was shattered by the desperate cry of the fowl community at this unprovoked attack from above.

Every animal in the courtyard instinctively dived into the nearest safe hiding hole. The chicken, the hens and even Bunki the COCKEREL of the house all hastily found a niche to dodge into, to escape the menace from the sky.

The marauding hawk was frightened away by the noise and clamour raised by all the gathered members of the fowl community. The most senior of Bunki's wives, Manya, reacted angrily to her husband's obvious cowardice in the face of danger.

"You cowardly, no good, spineless, useless cockerel. Imagine running, stumbling over everything in fear of another male like you. That hawk that just came, is he any older than you? You couldn't even stand up to it and defend your family like any virile male would do, instead you ran away without shame. Bunki shame on you! It's only when it comes to us, your wives and children, that you want to act tough."

She clapped her hands insolently and jeered at him. Old Bunki looked at his wife, Manya, for some time and then shook his head sadly.

"Look my dear, what you don't understand is that the fright that animal gave me when I was a chicken is still in me. That I ran was instinctive, not out of fear."

Manya was speechless, not knowing what to say next. She realised that she too went into hiding only because from childhood, she was made to believe that that was the only option with the hawks. Her parents too never taught her it was possible to put up a fight against the hawk.

After a while Manya said: "Next time, we shouldn't go into hiding. That's why he keeps coming to terrorise us, seeing we run away at the sight of him. Next time, we should all go out and fight."

Bunki agreed. "We must fight the fear. I can't see one stupid hawk winning over all of us – claw for claw and beak-for-beak."

20

The blind man and the lame man

Obong Udak was the king of Uwan. He was a very powerful ruler. Every one in the land feared him because he owned all the farmland in the village. All the goats, cattle, sheep and chicken in the village also belonged to him.

Anyone in the land who wished to eat any type of food – yam, corn, or even meat had to buy it from the king. While Udak and his coterie grew fat and happy, the rest of the villagers were all emaciated and unhappy. Everyone feared complaining about the king's greed and selfishness as such would lead to the arrest of the person, severe beating, a jail term or even the person being sold into slavery. Udak was extremely powerful because in addition to being the king, he was also the chief priest of the great oracle of the land of Uwan.

At this time in Uwan, lived two men, Uwem and Etim. Uwem was blind while Etim was lame in his two legs and therefore couldn't walk at all. These two men, who were respectively visually and physically challenged from birth, were good friends.

In a land where able- bodied men, who had no form of disability at all, found it difficult to find food, the problem faced by Uwem and Etim in finding food could only be imagined.

One day, after a long period of going without any food, the two hungry friends decided to do something about their plight. They decided to go and steal corn from the king's corn farm.

There was however a severe law in the land against stealing. If anyone lost any item, the person would report it to the chief priest of the oracle, that is, to Udak, who would in turn consult the oracle. The oracle would in turn summon everyone in the land to its shrine. There each person would swear his or her innocence. Anyone, whom the oracle pronounced guilty, would instantly die. If however the oracle did not find any one guilty of the crime in question, it would kill the complainant for levelling false accusations.

Despite their knowledge of the existence of the draconian law, the two desperately hungry friends continued to scheme on how to carry out their plans.

On the night of the agreed burglary, Uwem the blind one, carried Etim the cripple, on his back as they made for the king's corn farm. Uwem was giving Etim directions and when they got to the farm, it was again Uwem who plucked the ripe corns and put them into their big bag. By the time they had filled their sack, they had plucked nearly all the ripe corns in the farm. After this, they left for their homes with their loot, unspotted by anyone.

In the morning, the king discovered the burglary on his farm and raised an alarm. No one of course came forward to admit to the crime. Therefore after some days of waiting for the culprits to come forward, Udak summoned the whole village to the oracle's shrine for oath-taking.

When the entire village had gathered, the first man stepped forward.

"I Ekpo Ekong, the son of Udo Umoh swear by the great oracle, that, I did not steal any corn from Obong Udak's farm. If I am telling lies, may the oracle kill me."

After saying that, the man stepped over the calabash of concoction placed in front of the oracle. Successfully crossing over the calabash meant he was not found guilty.

Another man stepped forward, swore and crossed over the calabash. So did many others, until it came to the turns of Etim and Uwem. Uwem the blind one went first.

"I am Uwem Uwem," he declared. "I swear by the oracle that since my mother gave birth to me, that my two eyes have never beheld, Obong Udak's corn farm. If not so, may the oracle punish me horribly." He crossed over.

Then came the turn of the lame Etim, who also declared that since his mother gave birth to him that his two legs had never walked into the farmland of Obong Udak. "Mighty oracle, if I am lying, may you take my life this minute," he said and then crossed over the calabash – successfully.

At the end of the oath taking, the oracle observed that the two clever thieves had out-witted the wicked king, for, as Uwem had never seen the farm, and Etim had never walked to the farm, none of them could be held liable for the burglary.

The oracle was so angry with Obong Udak for having caused so much suffering and hunger to his people that they were forced to resort to stealing in order to eat. The oracle therefore killed Udak, and liberated the entire people of his kingdom from his despotism. Etim and Uwem were to this day treated as heroes in Uwan for spurring their liberation from Udak's dictatorship.

21

The mother hen's story

The king had an only son, whom he loved most passionately. He took him everywhere he went. He was his father's pride and joy.

One day the young prince fell ill. The king immediately sent for the palace physician. After examining the sick prince, the doctor unfortunately could not say exactly what was wrong with him. Without wasting time, another great doctor was sent for. The doctor came with speed, but alas, he too could not diagnose the young prince's malady.

The king was terribly worried.

Other famous physicians came and tried their best, but to no avail. Young doctors came and tried without any success. Doctors from distant lands came but none of them could help the ailing prince. The sickness beat the knowledge of the best physicians. The health of the prince meanwhile continued to deteriorate.

At last the deeply worried king consulted the oracle. For days the frightened king waited for the verdict of the oracle. What could be wrong with his only son? Why couldn't he get well, even after being attended to by the best physicians in the land?

Eventually the priest of the oracle emerged. The king rushed to him.

"What did the oracle say?" he inquired anxiously. But the old priest shook his head sadly. He was too upset to speak. Tears ran down his wizened, painted cheeks. At last he spoke. "The gods want your son, oh king."

That night the young prince died.

The king was devastated. He wept like a baby, tore his robe and poured red sand over his head, beard and body. His sorrow was deep. Why did the gods decide to deal him such a terrible blow? What did he do to deserve all these? No one could answer the distraught king's heart-rending questions.

In his sorrow the king went into his inner chamber and locked himself in. He refused to come out despite attempts by his household and the court to make him realise that life must go on. The elders of the land were summoned. They went and appealed to the king through the closed door's hole to consider his people and come out. They told him that matters concerning the land were suffering because of his decision to lock himself there. The king did not respond. He ignored them and continued grieving.

Neighbouring kings and royalties who came to pay their condolences went back home without seeing the grieving king.

His subjects got very worried. Seven days passed without the king eating any food. The whole village, including animals, gathered in the village square to consider what to do. The hen was in the crowd. She was however busy scratching, clucking, pecking and feeding with her children, very uninterested in the gathering or the reason for the meeting. When, at a point one animal queried the hen on why she did not seem to be concerned about the king's grief, the hen replied curtly: "If the man wants to die, why not allow him to die. After all, he is not the first to lose a child; neither will he be the last."

This comment attracted the attention of all gathered, including the king who locked himself inside his innermost chamber.

Many people and animals reacted very angrily to the hen's insensitive remark. Some fanatical supporters of the king tried to lynch her but the wise old owl stopped them. He then asked the hen to explain why she had made such an insensitive comment about the grieving king when every other person and animal in the land was showing their   concern and sympathy with the king.

It was then that the hen raised her voice and addressed the gathering, including the king.
 She said:

Oh king, come out and eat
Come out and eat oh king
If you think, you have a problem
Then listen to the story of my life.
My misery starts from my first day on earth.
As an egg, every table that wants to have a
good meal must have an egg.
And that includes you oh king.

Any native doctor that wants his medicine
to be potent will need an egg. Every careless
goat, sheep, horse or mule tramples on my eggs
with impunity and without feeling any qualms.

Thieving dogs and angry snakes feed on eggs.
If I survive this and become a chick, I become a
 prey to the hawk and the kite.

Then when I become a full adult bird,

every table again needs me for meal.
Again, every kind of native doctor and
oracle priest demand me for their work to
be effective.
Every ceremony and occasion is successful,
only after the fowl's blood and flesh have been
mutilated, cannibalised and wasted.
Every carnivorous, marauding bush cat
uses my family for food.

The fowl, unlike many others,
has no naturally- endowed defence
against these hazards of life. I am a woman
with a sad story of life.
I have suffered loss of loved ones.
I see my children being murdered everyday.
My brothers and sisters are chased and
slaughtered in my presence.

I endure the humiliation of people pointing
at me whenever a festival draws near.
No member of my family has ever been known
to die of old age. Meanwhile I stand aside and
watch the mischievous cat being treated as royalty
and the terrible dog doted upon. I do not complain.

So, oh king, come out and eat,
for the loss of one child is not the end of life.
Watch me, the mother hen, with my long line of losses.
Yet every day I come out and greet the morning sun
with a cluck, take whatever remains of my children
and walk proudly, with my head held high,
not knowing if that is my last day.

My husband, despite man's and animal's cruelty

 to his family, heralds the morning with loud crows.
Happy for every day he survives.
Come out and eat oh king, for your loss is not the most.
The ill fate of life is worst visited on the fowl.

When the mother hen has finished rendering her very
moving story, there was silence. Then slowly the door
of the king's inner chamber cracked open, and the king
emerged.
He then asked for food, and change of cloth. The king
from then on bore his loss with fortitude, inspired by
the wise words of the mother hen.

22

The lion cub and the lamb

The lion cub was in the forest square playing. He was chasing a little *udara* fruit he had picked up by the stream path. He was frolicking all over the square, laughing merrily and enjoying himself.

Suddenly the lamb, mama sheep's little boy, appeared. The lamb stood watching the lion's boy having fun. After a while, he joined him. The cub threw the fruit to him; he caught it and threw it back. They chased the *udara* fruit all over the square, enjoying themselves. Many times, they fell over each other, laughing and rolling all over the sand of the square, their innocent, merry glee ringing from one end of the square to the other, bouncing off trees and echoing all over.

The lioness, the lion cub's mama, came out of her house, a little worried about the noise filtering to her from outside. She saw her boy playing with the lamb. Silently, she fumed, angry with her son for playing with the lamb instead of killing and bringing him home for their supper. "Doesn't the silly little boy know it is the sheep and her children, that they eat for meals," she murmured to herself.

Also mama sheep came out and saw her boy playing with the dangerous lion's son. She was distraught and very afraid. She kept on watching from her hiding place and praying that the little lion would do no harm to her son. Eventually the playing, innocent friends got tired and hungry. They had played happily until sunset. They decided to go home, after agreeing to meet again the following day.

When the little lion cub got home however, his mother gave him a vicious cuff behind the ear. She dragged him by the ear into the house and smacked him soundly. "Did you not know that the lamb you let go today is a delicacy in this house? Well, that was your supper that you just let go, so go to bed, there will be no supper for you." The frightened little lion went to bed, sad and hungry.

When the lamb got home also, his mother could not hold herself. She smacked his hindside mercilessly. She admonished him seriously: "How dare you play with the child of the lion? Don't you know they kill us for food? Never you try that again, do you hear me? Never you go near that cub again, not to talk of playing with him!"

The following day the little lion boy, hungry and aware of what his mother had told him came out to the square, quite early in the noontime, to wait for the lamb to come to play with him, so that he could kill him. The cub waited for hours but the young lamb did not show up.

Much later, after the cub had waited in vain for several hours, he saw the lamb passing in the distance. The cub called him, "Come my friend, let us play, like we did yesterday," he said, trying to sound very friendly. But the wary little lamb kept his safe distance. As the young lion continued to persuade him, the young lamb, from a very safe distance, shouted back: "That thing your mother told you about us, my mother also told me about you lions." With that, he broke into a fast run, and did not look back until he got home.

23

The eagle that became a chicken

One day a shepherd took his sheep to the top of the mountain to graze on the fresh, green grass there. There he saw a dead eagle. It had been shot by hunters, and had flown to her nest to die.

In the eagle's nest, the shepherd found an egg the eagle was incubating before she was shot. The shepherd took both the dead eagle and the egg home. He gave the eagle to his wife to cook and the egg he took to where one of his hens was incubating her own eggs.

The shepherd put the eagle's egg among the hen's own eggs, hoping that the hen would incubate the eagle's egg while incubating hers, and that she would also hatch the egg when it became time to hatch her own.

Some days later, the eggs were hatched, including the eagle's egg. The eaglet grew up with the chickens and foraged for dirt and crumbs with the other chickens that she thought were her siblings. The eaglet did not know that she was actually an offspring of the Queen of the birds, and that she was not supposed to eat dirt and scratch the rough earth in search of food like the chickens.

One day, while the eaglet was outside playing with her siblings, she looked up and saw the eagle soaring gracefully in the sky. She stopped playing and watched with awe as an eagle hovered above with impressive confidence and majesty. Later the eaglet went to the hen she believed was her mother and asked: "What's that beautiful majestic bird soaring confidently in the sky?"

The hen told her that the bird she saw was an eagle, the Queen of the birds. "A mere chicken like you can never get to be an eagle," the hen scolded, meaning to impress it on the eaglet that it would be a waste of time day-dreaming about being like the eagle. The eaglet sighed in disappointment and went back to play, believing what her mother, the hen had told her.
So the eagle lived and died as a chicken, not actually knowing she was an offspring of the Queen of the birds.

24

The fox and the dog

Once upon a time, there was famine in the land of the animals. All the animals were going everywhere, searching for food. They were all hungry. The fox was one of the worst hit.

The fox was known for his slenderness. With many days of going without food, he looked bony and scraggy. He looked extremely tired and moved about in shuffles. His face had a permanent sad countenance.

One day while foraging desperately for food, the fox wandered farther than he had ever done. He came to a very high fence and stopped. Coming from the other side of the fence was the wonderful aroma of fresh meat. Quickly the hungry fox began to think of a way to cross the fence. Eventually he found a small hole in the fence. He continued to scratch and paw on it until the hole was large enough for him to pass through. He then crawled through the hole on his belly to the other side.

He emerged into a beautiful, well looked after compound. However before he could get his bearing, there was the loud and menacing bark of a dog somewhere in the compound. The fox froze and was about to scamper back through the hole, when his stomach rumbled, reminding him that he had not eaten for some days. He therefore decided to stand his ground and withstand any vicious dog; if victory in such an encounter would mean that he could get to the meat he had smelt.

The barking became louder and more menacing. The fox luckily was able to clearly locate the direction of the barking and quickly sneaked off in the opposite direction. Then he tried to trace the source of the delicious meat whose aroma made his mouth water. To his dismay however, he observed that the aroma of the meat was oozing from the same direction as the dog's bark. The fox was momentarily distraught. But he was so desperately hungry that he was ready to take any risk for food.

He began to crawl slowly to the direction from which the aroma of the meat and the dog's barks were coming from. Suddenly he came face to face with a very large, fierce-looking dog. The fox swallowed hard, but bravely stood his ground. His desire for food was obviously stronger than his fear. The dog was taken aback at this lack of fear by the fox and it showed on his face. This emboldened the fox.

As he got closer to the dog, he also found to his surprise that the dog did not look especially tough or strong, only fat and well fed. The intrepid fox took all these in one glance. But what captivated his attention was a fat bone lying in front of the dog.

He thought hard on how to get to the bone without making himself an easy prey to the dog. An idea dropped into his mind: "Hello brother doggie," he greeted. "How are we this great and beautiful day?" he asked, looking up at the sky.

The dog said nothing.
"No need to ask," continued the sly fox. "I can see that you are quite great. I just wish you could have sometimes made out the time to attend the animals' meetings. By now you would have been the king of the

animals instead of that scraggy, mean, cruel and unreliable lion. You would like that, eh?" He looked at the dog slyly, while slowly moving towards the bone.
"Ehm ehm," the gullible dog was lost for words.

"You have all it takes, I tell you - a good background, good character, good credentials. Only what you need now is for an eloquent someone like me to nominate you for that position."
"Well, mm, hem ehm…" the confused dog was still tongue-tied.
"You see the animals look up to great ones like you. All you have to do is give them pieces of bones like this one." He gave the bone a little tap. " Surely, you can spare this, can't you?" asked the fox with a rue smile.
"Oh yes, of course, they can have it."

"Oh, then I can have this, they can have any others that follow. I want to make sure it is a good piece of bone." He immediately ate up the bone.

The dog was pleased. He went into his kernel and fetched more bones. The fox packed the bones into a bundle and dragged the bundle with him to the forest.

This was the beginning of a good friendship between the fox and the dog. The fox visited the dog everyday, and on each occasion the dog made bundles of bones, which he took with him back to the forest.

The lucky fox began to look well fed and happy. His fine brown coat developed a luxuriant shine, and his tail with its white tip became quite full and wavy.
The fox lauded the dog's good fortune of having a good home and abundant food supply at a time of terrible famine and austerity for all the other animals. He never tired of reminding the dog how lucky he was.

One day the fox invited the dog to a party organised by the animals. The fox told him that every animal wanted to meet him to show their appreciation for all the food he had been sending to them. He told the dog the animals planned to honour him for his benevolence and generosity.

The fox observed that the dog was uneasy with the invitation. "What is it?" he asked.

The dog looked at the fox solemnly, then pointed at the collar around his (dog's) neck. He asked the confused fox if he knew the meaning of the collar.

The fox did not know.

The dog then explained that the collar on his neck was the price he had to pay for the nice home and abundant food supply he had. The collar, he continued, was to be a constant reminder of the restrictions imposed on him by his master in exchange for food and a home.

The fox was shocked. "Do you mean, that you are not allowed to go out and come back at will? Not even to attend a party organised by your fellow animals?"

"Yes, that is right," the dog replied.

The fox shook his head in disbelief. He wasn't sure if he would be happy to trade positions with the dog. He looked again at the dog and realised how sad he was. "Was that why he barked the way he did?" he murmured to himself. As he returned to the forest, he suddenly realised how lucky he was to have to the freedom to move or run as he pleased, and talk to whoever he wished to. He resolved that at the animals' party, he would bring up the question of how to help the poor dog.

25

The antelope and his antlers

Ligo the antelope had a pair of extremely beautiful antlers. They were curvy, branched and brightly coloured. Ligo was extremely proud of his beautiful antlers. Nothing gave him as much pleasure as going to the stream and gazing for hours at the reflection of his antlers on the water.

Whenever Ligo walked, he had a way of tossing his head from left to right, showing off his beautiful antlers. If any animal wished to get any favours from him, all the animal had to do was pay compliments to his antlers. Ligo was, to put it simply, very obsessed with his antlers.

Ligo's only regrets were his feet. For Ligo, they were so tiny and thin that he constantly felt conscious of them. He was so ashamed of his feet that when he took a walk, he often did so among the tall grasses so that his feet would not be seen. Whenever he went to the stream to drink water and meet other animals there, he would quietly sneak into the water in an effort to hide his tiny legs. But he never missed any opportunity to show off his beautiful antlers.

During festivals and ceremonial occasions, Ligo liked to deck his antlers with all sorts of flowers and colourful creepers. One wise gnu, which lived in the thick forest, once frankly told Ligo that he was getting his priorities mixed up. He advised him to pay more attention to his feet as they were the greatest asset nature endowed an antelope with in the rough life of the jungle. But Ligo never listened.

One day, as Ligo was wandering through the forest, a sharp thorn stuck into his hoof but he did not pay it much heed, instead he was more concerned with chasing away flies from his beautiful antlers. Then suddenly Ligo heard the fearful sounds of barking hounds. Hunters were approaching. Immediately Ligo, despite the thorn in his hoof, took off in a graceful and splendid galloping. The feet, which he had always underestimated, even undermined, performed their duty diligently. Effortlessly they carried the antelope across the dense forest, safely away from the hunters.

When he thought he was out of danger and was beginning to relax, disaster struck. The great, beautiful, colourful, splendid, highly admired antlers got caught and entangled in the low foliage of the forest. That was where the hunting dogs caught up with Ligo. As the antelope was dying, he deeply regretted all the attention he paid to his antlers, for despite the efforts he put in caring for it, the antlers still turned out to be his undoing.

26

The lion is ill

Old Mungo the lion, king of the animals, had become too old to go out to hunt for food. He had become too weak to go and hunt in the jungle like he used to do in his younger days.

Crafty old Mungo therefore worked out a plan with his friend Kwura, the hyena. Their aim was simple – find a way to get food without having to go hunting. In other words, they wanted to find a way of making their food come to them.

Kwura went to the jungle and announced that their beloved king, the Old Mungo, had fallen ill and was dying. Kwura said the king instructed that he wanted to have a private audience with the animals. He wanted to bless each and every one of them before his death.

Most of the animals were deeply moved by the king's illness and the disheartening news that he was about to move to the world beyond. They therefore all trooped to the lion's den to pay their last respect to him. The hyena however deterred them. He suggested that since the King wanted to spend considerable time with each animal, it was best that they all came at different times and days. The animals agreed. So one day, it would be the turn of the antelope, another day that of the goat, then the sheep, followed by the chicken, and so forth.

This continued for many days, until it got to the monkey's turn. The suspicious monkey got to the tree in front of the lion's lair. He peered into the entrance and shook his head. He had, from the beginning, been distrustful of this lion-hyena partnership.

"Well, come on, hurry up, the king does not have to wait for you all day, he has others to see, you know," the hyena urged him. Again the intelligent monkey shook his head. He pointed at the entrance to the den. "There are so many foot prints going into the den, but none coming out," he told the hyena.

"Ehm ehm, you see, actually, the fact is… what I am trying to say is ehm," the confused hyena stuttered on.

"Well, obviously the place will be quite filled up with animals. So I will come and pay my respect to the king when those inside have come out," he said, and swung from that tree to another.

27

The frog and some naughty children

One day, some children playing outside saw one frog moping at them. One cheeky boy suggested that they should catch it, which they did. It happened back in the days when animals spoke human language.

The naughty children formed two lines with a circle drawn on the ground in between. They took turns in tossing Mister frog as high as they could so as to see which group could get him to fall into the small circle in the centre.

At each throw, the children would shout excitedly and happily. They were having so much fun.

"Oh Mister frog," they yelled, "you are so much fun to play with." And up would go Mister frog again only to land once more on the hard ground.

The children got particularly excited after an especially high throw in which the unfortunate frog landed on his head. "Oh Mister frog, we hope that did not hurt?" the children teased. They were eager to repeat this high throw and hard landing once more.

"Well, well," said the bruised and battered frog, "I hope you kids are enjoying yourselves?'

"Yes, yes," they chorused.

"Well you, see my children," he said to them, "this show you are regarding as fun for yourselves, for me, it signals my death."

28

The inquisitive lion cub

Muzakah was the son of Zimba, the lion. He was a curious, inquisitive and an adventurous little one. He asked too many questions and wanted to know the answer to all the riddles that worried his infant mind.

If Muzakah saw a mountain, he would demand to know from his mother, Mizat, why the mountain was that high. If he saw the birds soaring in the sky, he would want to know why. He wanted answers to such questions as: Why were birds able to fly? And why couldn't he fly like the birds? At the spring where the family fetched their drinking water from, Muzakah wanted to know what was at the depth of the water.

To all his questions, his mother had a simple answer: "Patience my little brave one, when you grow up, you will find out the answer to all your questions." But restless Muzakah felt that his mother's answers were rather too patronising. He decided therefore to go and find the answers to the numerous questions bothering him. One evening, after his parents had gone hunting for food, Muzakah left their lair, and headed for the spring. Immediately he came out of the den, he ran onto Jumbo, the elephant, who nearly trampled him with his heavy foot. Muzakah luckily escaped death.

He continued along the track, and suddenly a tiger snarled at him, and chased him quite a distance up the track before letting him go.

The panting little Muzakah took a turn to the right and *bang!* It was the mean Bunkea, the rhinoceros. It snorted fiercely and charged the little lion cub, nearly goring it. Muzakah nimbly jumped out of the way of the charging bully, lost his balance and fell. He rolled down a steep slope and ended up in a muddle in the swamp where the spring was. He had mud in his eyes, mouth and ears and was spitting and coughing. Little Muzakah was dragging himself out of the swamp when, *snap, snap*, Aguiyi, the crocodile, whose siesta he had disturbed by his noisy arrival, came after him. Ill-tempered and grouchy, its wide mouth and mighty teeth came after the little cub, *snap snap*. Hastily little Muzakah clambered unto the bank.

He sat there for quite a while, panting. He felt quite small and frightened. Eventually he painfully dragged himself up and fearfully started crawling home, diving into the nearest bush at any little noise. By the time he got home, it was quite late.

His worried mother saw him, and rushed out to hug him. "What happened to you son, where did you wander off to? You look quite hurt," she said, worried at the mud all over her son and the frightened look on his face. The poor boy shook his head sadly. "It is a jungle out there, mummy," he said. "We are living among very wild animals. This neighbourhood is not safe for peace-loving folks like us, lions." Mizat looked at her son for a long time, shook her head and smiled.

She patted his head affectionately and told him to get into the den, clean himself up and eat his supper. "One day, when you have grown up, you will find the answers," she cajoled him. In her mind however, she was thinking: "You will know son that you will be like your father and mother, the wildest and strongest animal in the jungle. You will also discover the irony of what you just said about wild animals making the jungle unsafe for peace-loving animals like us. I am sure it is exactly what other mothers tell their children concerning us."

29

Haruna and the camel

Haruna was a poor trader. He owned only one camel, which he used to carry his goods to the market. Haruna usually travelled to very distant markets to sell his wares. He therefore depended solely on his camel for his livelihood. Because Haruna and his camel travelled to very far places for his business dealings, sometimes they had to spend the night along the road, or in thick forests, depending on where the night caught up with them. In such situations, Haruna would just pitch his tent and spend the night inside the tent while the camel would sleep outside, beside the tent.

One day while Haruna and his camel were coming back from a very distant market, they had to cross the great wide desert. The desert got very hot during the day, when the sun was up, but extremely cold at nights, when the sun had gone down.

Haruna hurried his camel on so that the night would not catch up with them in the arid desert. Besides the desert being extremely cold at nights, there were also frequent sandstorms and Haruna especially dreaded it.

The camel became very tired after walking for a very long distance without rest, and constantly being hurried by Haruna. After a while he refused to be hurried no matter how much the worried Haruna cajoled, threatened or even beat him. Eventually, it got dark, and they could not continue with the journey, as they could no longer see where they were going. Haruna therefore had to find somewhere for them to spend the night. He saw a large sand dune, and decided to pitch his tent beside it, so that it would shield them from the blast of the sandstorm. He knew however that that would not protect them from the intense cold of the desert night.

Haruna was hungry and thirsty. He wished he could locate an oasis - a fertile place in the desert, where they could at least find some water, and with some luck, date palms to eat. Unfortunately, it was too dark so searching for such an oasis was out of the question. He therefore pitched his tent, and went inside to sleep, leaving the camel outside, as usual.

Soon Haruna, who was also very tired, slept off. It was not long, however, when he started feeling a nudge on him. He woke up to see that it was the camel. "What is it?" he asked the camel irritably.

To Haruna's utter surprise the camel spoke. "Please, Master Haruna, my head is very cold. Can I just stick it into the tent, so that it doesn't freeze, lest I die of cold." Despite his surprise, Haruna reasoned that if the camel died he would not have any means of getting out of the desert.

"All right, bring your head into the tent." He said and went back to sleep.

Soon afterwards, he felt another nudge. Again, he woke up. "What is it this time?" Haruna, snoring away in deep slumber, was quite irritated.

"Please sir, it is my chest. The cold has caught up with it. I can hardly breathe. Can I please bring my poor chest into the tent so that it can get warm," the camel requested, shivering with cold. Haruna looked around the little tent, assessing its ability to contain him and the camel's chest. Shrugging, he said: "All right, all right," and promptly went back to sleep, as the big camel brought his big chest inside the tent.

A little while afterwards, the sleeping Haruna again felt a stronger push and shake. He woke up with a start, thinking that they had come under an attack only to discover it was once again the camel.

Haruna was exasperated. 'What is the matter with you?" he asked angrily. "What again do you want from me that you cannot allow me to sleep?"

"Sorry for disturbing you, Master Haruna. It is my poor tummy. I think the cold has entered into it. It is swelling up. If I leave it outside for another minute, it will freeze and I will die." The camel sobbed, tears dribbling down his cheeks. Haruna took compassion on him and allowed him to drag his great belly into the tent.

The tent was meant to accommodate only one person so when the camel dragged his belly into the tent, Haruna became uncomfortably squeezed. He could no longer sleep. It was not long again before the camel started fidgeting. Haruna demanded to know from him what the problem was. The camel said his hind legs were both frozen and that he was afraid he might not walk again because he could no longer feel anything on them. He then asked if he could bring them into the tent to see if it would help. Furious, Haruna firmly said "No." The camel started crying and weeping bitterly. He asked Haruna to remember all his selfless services to him in the past. Haruna ignored him. Then the pesky camel changed tactics. He reminded Haruna that if he let him die in the desert that he, Haruna, would not have any means of leaving the wide unfriendly desert. The camel urged

Haruna to save him so as to save himself too. With this argument Haruna capitulated and allowed the camel to bring in his hind legs into the tents.

As soon as Haruna allowed the camel to bring his hind legs into the tent, he was squeezed out of the tent because the little tent could only accommodate one person at a time. Haruna was therefore forced to leave the tent. After a while he began to beg the camel to let him into the tent because he was freezing outside.

But the camel refused. He cried and begged the camel like the camel did to him, but the camel refused to pay him any heed. The only time the camel talked to him was to ask him to move further away from the tent because his (Haruna's) pleas and cries were disturbing his sleep.

30

Yusuf and the donkey

In a village by the great lake, lived a man called Yusuf. Yusuf was a trader. He bought salt from traders who got it from the lake and then resold it in the big market with profit.

Yusuf had a donkey, which carried the salt for him from the lake to the city market. Salt is normally heavy and Yusuf usually bought a lot, which the donkey would be made to carry to the market. The donkey, of course, did not like this, and often tried to shed some of the load on the way to the market. The donkey resorted to all sorts of tricks to do this. Sometimes it would pretend to have broken a leg and would start limping. At other times it would pretend to be ill and would refuse to get up in the morning or would deliberately fall down on its way to the market and would pretend to be dead. But Yusuf was never taken in by any of those tricks.

Every one along the market route knew Yusuf and his naughty donkey.

On the way to the market was an old rickety wooden bridge. Yusuf and his obstinate donkey had to cross this bridge to, and from the market. Each time Yusuf and his donkey got to this bridge, the donkey would refuse to cross. Yusuf would scold and plead but the donkey would remain adamant until Yusuf brought out the whip. Only then would the donkey reluctantly cross over.

One day it rained very heavily and the rickety old bridge was very slippery. The donkey found this a comfortable excuse not to cross the bridge. But Yusuf insisted that they must cross since it was necessary to get to the market to sell their salt. The donkey refused to set foot on the tottery bridge. Yusuf threatened the donkey verbally but it still did not budge. So Yusuf had no alternative than to resort to his normal method of whipping the donkey. He flogged the obstinate donkey several times before it decided to give the bridge a trial.

Because the donkey was very afraid and shaking all over, when it got to the middle of the bridge, it lost its balance and fell into the river, with the bags of salt it was carrying. Yusuf, without any hesitation, dived into the river and promptly rescued his donkey. But alas, he could not save his salt, as it had all melted in the water. When he brought the donkey to the ground, the animal observed with surprise that its load had become lighter. It laughed noisily and nodded its head wisely. "So a dive into the river makes one's load lighter," it thought with a happy grin.

The next time they were going to the market, much to every one's surprise, the normally recalcitrant and uncooperative donkey was hurrying. Yusuf thought that its fall into the river might have cured the animal of its obstinacy. But he was in for a rude shock, for as soon as they got to the bridge; the donkey promptly dived into the river. Yusuf was infuriated. He dived into the river and saved the donkey, but alas, he lost his salt a second time. He beat the mischievous donkey mercilessly. But it looked unrepentant.

The next time they were going to the market, the donkey was again planning its trick. As they approached the old bridge, it took off at a brisk trot, still bearing its heavy load. Yusuf followed it. Immediately the donkey got to the bridge, it took a dive into the water. The patient Yusuf dived after it into the river for the third time and rescued it. They continued their journey to the market.

The donkey was however very surprised that instead of the weight of its load lightening as a result of the dive into the river, it had increased four times. The donkey did not know that the clever Yusuf, instead of buying salt this time, had bought sponge. So instead of melting like the salt does, the sponge had soaked more water and increased its weight four times.

The donkey learnt its lessons. From then, each time it got to the bridge, it would cross it gently and carefully, not knowing what it was carrying, whether it was something its weight would lighten or quadruple with a dive into the river.

31

The ant and the grasshopper

The ant was a busy, hard-working little insect. It was difficult to see him relaxing. At anytime, he was either hurrying home with some foods or rushing off to somewhere to collect more food.

Mister ant and his family lived in a hole. All through the dry season, when the weather was usually fine, he would stock his foods in the hole. When the hole was full, such that there was no longer any space for Mister ant and his large family to live in it, they would close that hole with dry leaves and seal it with saliva. Then they would leave a mark such as a piece of wood or leaves in the place to help them identify it in future. The ant and his family would then make another hole, which they would immediately start filling up with food.

The ant had a friend, Mister grasshopper, who lived in the nearby cornfield. He lived on the stalks of the corn, and fed on the grains. He neither gathered food nor stored grains for the rainy season, when it would normally be difficult to do so. He liked to chirp merrily all day long, flying from one corn stalk to another and generally feeling quite happy with himself. He never seemed to worry about anything in the world.

One day, the ant, his friend, called him and advised him to start gathering food because the rainy season was fast approaching and he suspected the farmer would soon come to harvest his corn. But the foolish grasshopper told him that the cornfield was too large, and that he was sure no one could harvest all the corn in the field. The grasshopper insisted there was enough corn in the field for everyone for many years. The wise ant pointed out that the cornfield was not his but the farmer's, and that one day the owner was bound to come and harvest his corns. The grasshopper laughed merrily, and with a smile of superior wisdom, said he knew how to reap where he did not sow. He also blamed the ant for his large family, and told him that his large family had meant that he (the ant) had to work all the time without having any time for pleasure.

The grasshopper liked to boast of his foresight, especially his decision to be a bachelor and not saddle himself with many obligations. He would, he said, never trade his freedom for anything in the world and sympathised with the ant for not having as much foresight as he, the grasshopper. He further boasted that he could provide for himself and therefore needn't worry; and strongly recommended that the ant should make out time to get a life, adding philosophically that all *work and no play would make Okeke a dull boy*. The ant replied that, "all play and no work would also make Okeke a dull boy."

The grasshopper remained nonchalant, and continued with his carefree way of life.

Then the rains came.

One day the owner of the farm came with his family to harvest the corn. The grasshopper was briefly worried as he watched the farmer and his family cutting the corn stalks. But soon he got carried away and started chirping away noisily. Each time the farmer got to the corn stalks where he was perching, the grasshopper would fly away to another stalk, chirping merrily. The children of the farmer chased him from stalk to stalk as he flew about, enjoying himself.

Soon the sun went down, and the farmer and his family had to go, without cutting up to half of the corn in the field. The grasshopper watched them go, and laughed. He called out to his friend, the ant, and said: "Didn't I tell you. No one can cut all the corn in this field." But the wise ant just said to him: "We wait and see." And he went on with his busy activities. The grasshopper looked at him and shook his head regrettably. "Poor Mister ant, he does not have the time to enjoy his life," he mused.

The next day, the farmer and his people came back and harvested half of the field. The grasshopper again watched them, again he watched them go and again he laughed and went to sleep.

The rain continued. The farmer continued his harvesting. One day it rained so heavily that the normally nonchalant grasshopper got worried. Then matters got worse for him as the the farmer came back next day with a lot of others and they harvested all the corn. By that time the ant and his family had retired into their hole and covered it securely against the rains. The grasshopper now had no shelter to cover him from the rains and no more corns for food. He started starving, and began to grow lean. His once beautiful feather, which he was so proud of, grew pale and colourless.

One day, the hungry grasshopper went to the mouth of the hole where his friend, the ant, lived and started knocking to be let in for shelter and food. It was raining heavily that day but the ant refused to open the door. The sick grasshopper continued knocking and calling on his friend to open the door and let him in but the ant ignored him. He felt he had warned his friend sufficiently that a stitch in time would save nine.

The knocking continued, until it grew feeble and eventually stopped. After many days, it stopped raining. The ant opened the door, and there was the dead body of his friend, the grasshopper. He called his children and showed them the body of his former friend, saying: "This is what happens to someone who does not take life seriously." They carried the carcass into the hole, and stored the dry dead body of the grasshopper among the food they were storing for the dry season.

Part 2
Idioms and proverbs

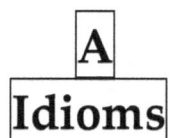

A
Idioms

32

Idioms

1. It is when you come close to someone that you can perceive the person's mouth odour.
   It is only when you get intimate with someone that you can find out the person's weaknesses, shortcomings and secrets.

2. The elders should teach the children that the vulture is not edible meat.
   The elders should guide the younger ones on the norms and traditions of their people.

3. The sheep says that it pays to mope.
   Silence is golden.

4. What the dog beholds and barks excitedly about, the sheep sees and keeps silent.
   What excites some people, others could regard casually.

5. At first sight the croaking toad looks like a tough animal.
   First impressions are sometimes wrong.

6. Something must have to touch the drum for it to speak.
   Actions have causes.

7. The little bird dancing in the bush path, its drummer must be somewhere in the bush.
   Be careful how you respond to some unexpected situations, they may be instigated.

8. If you wake up in the morning and the lizard chases you, better run for you do not know if it had grown teeth during the night.
   Unwarranted provocation from least expected persons should be responded to with caution.

9. The stomach does not allow the feet a resting chance.
   The need for food causes a man to labour and suffer.

10. The wayward eyes search out the wayward feet.
    It takes a thief to catch a thief.

11. The monkey's agility is most pronounced in a jungle where the trees are close to each other.
    A person's supposed prowess is often exaggerated by the availability of the necessary tools and enabling condition.

12. The anus farts and the face gets the slap.
    A case of the innocents suffering for an offence committed by others

13. When we urinate together it foams.
    Collective ideas make the problem easier to solve.

14. Do not be intimidated by a big - - -, it cannot make love to itself.
    Do not be intimidated by a big problem, it is not going to solve itself.

15. If you make love to an old woman and later disparage her, remember the urge will come again.
    If you treat an endearment with levity, you will lose it and will miss
    it some day.

16. If you kill the native doctor that brews protection portions for you, what about your detractors.
    If you chase away your friends, how will you cope with your enemies?

17. Even the most majestic eagle eats a dirty frog.
    The great and powerful sometimes do debasing things.

18. Let the hawk perch and let the eagle perch. That which refuses the other to perch, may its wings break.
    Live and let live.

19. It is not every rainfall that warrants the earthen pot being brought out to fetch the rainwater.
    It is not everything that one hears, that one has to

react to.

20. If a mad man comes to where you are taking
    your bath and runs off with your clothes,
    and you chase after him while still naked,
    folks will say that they saw two mad men
    running along the street.
    If you argue with a fool, then there are two fools
    arguing.

21. Where a cattle is tethered is where it feeds.
    Where a man works, is where he gets his wages.

22. The boy is the father of the man.
    The child will one day grow up to be an adult.

23. When a boy throws his father in the air, the
    wrapper will blind him.
    There is a harsh price to pay for disrespect.

24. He who has gathered ants-infested firewood
    has invited lizards to a party.
    He who goes looking for trouble should not
    complain at the consequences.

25. If a masquerade is still dancing when the
    drummers and other instrument players
    have stopped playing, then there is a need to
    investigate whether it is man or spirit that is
    behind the mask.
    This character is totally out of rhythm with the
    norms of the society.

26. Why struggle for the dogs' faeces? If you do
    get it, will you eat it?
    Why be a dog in a manger?

27. The goat that hangs around with the dog
    will one day learn how to eat faeces.
    Evil association corrupts good manners.

28. The rat that exposes itself to the rain just
    because the lizard does, when the rain dries
    off from the lizard's body, will it also dry off
    from the its own body?
    Beware of dangerous emulation.

29. When one finger touches oil, the oil will
    inevitably spread to the other fingers
    One bad apple spoils the whole bunch.

30. It is the person that you spent the night with
    that will know if you have mouth odour or
    not.
    *It is the person that is close to you that knows
    your secrets.*

31. It is only the husband of the woman with a
    broken waist that knows how he sleeps with
    her.
    *It is only close family members of a person who
    has a handicap that know best how the person
    copes with the disability.*

32. Grandmother's goat ate grandmother's yam.
    I have, out of mischief, unknowingly, destroyed

what is mine.

33. You can show me my brother but not my friend.
    People make their own friends

34. The squirrel and the rabbit constantly fight over nests that belong to neither.
    Some people like fighting over what does not belong to them.

35. Why take medicine for another man's headache.
    Why worry or fight over another man's problems.

36. If a snake swallows another, the tail of the snake it swallowed must always stick out of its mouth.
    Some crimes are impossible to cover up.

37. When the corpse starts to stink, the friend who is assumed closer to him than his brothers and sisters when he was alive will disappear.
    Do not think your friends will ever value you more than your siblings.

38. The drunken cock has not yet met the crazy hawk.
    The bully who constantly spoils for a fight will sooner than later meet his match.

39. He claims he does not eat rat meat, yet he shares the rat meat for his children with his

teeth.
He claims to abhor something yet he cannot keep away from that thing

40. One does not need to break the coconut to find out if there is water inside it. If you shake it, you will know if it has water in it.
There are often simple methods of finding out what one is looking for.

41. The river can only drown the person whom it feels his feet.
The trouble can only affect you if you are within the scope of its influence.

42. The lizard that falls from the tall *iroko* tree says that if no one will praise it, it will praise itself.
If you perform a daring feat and no one appreciates it, you have the right to congratulate yourself for that.

43. The man whose daughter is married to the lizard should get used to folks rushing to his house to tell him that his son- in-law has fallen from a tree.
If you are used to making acquaintances with questionable characters then you should get used to embarrassments.

44. Life to the water, life to the fish. May the water not dry, may the fish not die.
Let there be a symbiotic existence for all.

45. A man cannot claim that the birth of his child took him by surprise.
     Some situations give you time to prepare for their occurrence.

46. The great *eke* market is not aware that one individual did not come to the market.
     Some circumstances are far beyond the influence of one man.

47. No matter how noisy the market may be, if one shouts your name, you are bound to hear it.
     Selective perception.

48. The sheep that begets a ram is still childless.
     Some offspring are just not worth it. They are just sources of constant pains and sorrows to their parents.

49. The goat has entered the barn, eaten the yams and now you are hurrying to shut the door to the barn.
     Acting too late after the damage had been done.

50. It is after we have chased away the fox that we can now sit down to advise the chicken not to wander about in the night.
     First remove the danger before apportioning blames.

51. God drives away flies for the cow without a tail.
     Fate often intercedes for the helpless.

52. The snail says that it is only with a smooth
    tongue that he can that he can successfully
    glide through thorns.
    Charm offensives can often help one get out of
    complex situations.

53. What a man does for another man is
    tantamount to 'Please keep this for me'.
    A favour or evil done to a friend is often a debt
    that needs to be repaid.

54. Secure the land first before fighting for the
    yam seedlings to plant on it.
    Important things first

55. You can't expect me to marry a wife for you
    and also buy the bed on which you and your
    wife will sleep, otherwise you will also
    expect me to make her pregnant for you.
    If I allow you to depend on me to solve all your
    problems, you may soon lose sight of your own
    responsibilities.

56. "I don't want it, take all of it," may not be a
    sincere offer.
    Some gifts may not be as generous as they seem,
    or may not be motivated by as much altruism as
    the giver wants us to believe.

57. If the entire village cooks for Okoro, he will
    obviously not finish the food, but if Okoro
    cooks for the village, they will eat it all.
    One cannot expect to be at loggerheads with the
    entire community and emerge victorious.

58. Don't be like the proverbial musician, who is beating the drum, dancing to the music, applauding himself and at the same time picking the money that people toss at him.
Don't be a jack of all trade

59. The axe with a good handle is not sharp, and the sharp axe has no handle
No one is perfect or good in all areas of life.

60. A person I taught hunting, and goes hunting with, now turns around to say that my head looks like that of an animal.
Some assumed friends are very good at treachery.

61. The bush fowl once told her children: 'When you pick a bit of tuber, also pick a bit of roots, so that when the farmer harvests his tubers you will still have something to keep you going'.
It is wisdom to think of, and prepare oneself for the rainy day.

62. I have had enough is not supposed to cause a controversy.
My intention not to be involved any more should be respect. One should not be forced to participate in a relationship or any situation against his will.

63. Why worry for the bigheaded one, are you going to wear his hat for him.
Why do you worry so much over someone else's problems, do you intend to take them over?

64. A person who chooses to visit the anus should not express any disgust at meeting Mr faeces there.
A person who chooses to put himself in a compromising situation should not be surprised if he ends up being humiliated.

65. Once the rain has fallen on the ground, it cannot return again to the sky as rain.
Some situations are irreversible. Some hurts never heal.

66. A broken earthen pot can never be mended.
Some *soured relationships can never be mended again.*

67. The palm fruit that touches the ground has picked up dirt.
Some actions change the nature of relationships forever, especially those involving the betrayal of trust.

68. The rainwater that has collected in the pit of a broken pot is for the stray dog.
Some duties are beneath some people, and should be left to people most suitable to do them.

69. When the gourd of water is left outside for too long, the spirits will wash their hands in it. .
Procrastination often makes what would have been a simple task very complex in the end.

70. I invited you to join me for a meal of foo-foo and you washed your two hands, what do

you expect me, the owner of the meal to do?
Take a bath?
*Cautionary words to the visitor that is making
himself too comfortable, and the borrower that is
over using the borrowed item.*

71. What you call your dog is what it is.
    As you make your bed, so you lie on it.

72. One has to masticate well before one
    swallows.
    *One needs to make adequate preparations before
    one embarks on a project.*

73. To pluck the pepper one has to go round and
    round the plant. You do not climb it.
    Some tasks require patience and diplomacy

74. The snake that bites a tortoise has bitten only
    a hard shell.
    One attempting something that is futile.

75. What you seek in Sokoto could be in your
    shokoto.
    *That which you travel far and wide to search for
    could just be around the corner.*

76. The great iroko tree has fallen and a woman
    has scaled it at last.
    The mighty has fallen and became debased.

77. The lion is crippled and the deer has come to
    collect his debt.

When a mighty person is incapacitated, his
inferiors become emboldened to talk to him in
ways they would not otherwise have done.

78. The snake that is beheld by only one person
is a python.
*An incident witnessed only by one person is often
prone to exaggeration.*

79. If one succeeds in climbing an iroko tree, one
should utilise the opportunity to collect fresh
leaves, firewood and the eggs of the eagle.
For climbing an iroko tree is not a venture
one accomplishes every other day of one's
life.
*When you get to a lofty position, try to make the
best use of it, for you cannot count on getting to
such a high position always, or remaining there
for a very long time.*

80. A journey to the end of the earth starts with
your stepping out of your house.
*A journey of one thousand kilometres starts with
a single step.*

81. That the snake has shed its skin does not
mean that it has become harmless.
*That someone who has been mean and brutal all
his life, now says he has changed, for example by
becoming religious, does not mean that the
person is no longer incapable of being mean and
brutal.*

82. The headhunter does not allow one with
a sharp cutlass to stand behind him.

The criminally minded are often the most suspicious of people around them.

83. No, you do not call me a thief in a crowded market and come home to say you are sorry.
   A false accusation that is levelled in the public should also be apologised for, in that public.

84. No one teaches the rat, which unwittingly entered a snake's hole how to come out.
   Desperation often lends one wings.

85. The fly that does not listen to advice goes to the grave with the corpse.
   An obstinate person that does not listen to advice is sure to get into a messy situation sooner than later.

86. You do not collect water from the pot only to pour it into the river.
   Taking from the needy and giving it to someone who does not really need it.

87. The leopard must always be spotted.
   Some traits are genetically inherited and may therefore be difficult to change.

88. It is not that a man slept with your wife that is the main problem; it is what was said about you before the act.
   How were you assessed before they concluded to take what rightly belongs to you?

89. The best friend of the fisherman is the fish. The worst enemy of the fish is the fisherman.

Your best friend could be your worst enemy and vice versa.

90. The little ant that thinks that his mother is stupid often ends up in the belly of the chicken.
    Disobedience or foolishness has disastrous consequences.

91. The coward often survives the war.
    He who has fear in him often survives because he applies caution in his dealings.

92. The frog's mouth is often full of water.
    I am dumbfounded.

93. The corpse of someone's mother seems like a log of wood to strangers and others not affected by the bereavement.
    Folks are apathetic to another's problem.

94. The palm wine tapper does not say all that he sees from the top of the palm tree.
    It is not all that one sees that one reveals. A man must be able to keep secrets.

95. The snake is struggling to escape from the room and they say it is fighting wildly.
    A man is loudly protesting his innocence and they say that he is violent. Some folks are totally misunderstood.

96. If there is no vulture on a big occasion involving animal sacrifices, then there must be some problems in the land of the spirits.

> *The absence of certain key players on some important occasions means that there is big problem somewhere.*

97. The stalk laden with fully ripe corns is often bent.

    The wise ones are often humble and quiet.

98. Eneke the bird says that since men have learnt to shoot without aiming, he too has learnt to fly without perching.

    One has learnt how to live or accommodate unreliable or unpredictable associates.

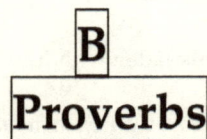

B
Proverbs

33

Proverbs

1. When a handshake goes beyond the elbow, it is tantamount to the declaration of a fight

2. As the ear has refused to hear, when the head is cut off, it goes with it too.

3. The world is as large as your knowledge of it.

4. What the young climbs the top of the tree to see, the old ones often know all about from the foot of the tree.

5. Twenty friends cannot remain friends for twenty years.

6. I can do it does not mean I will do it.

7. It is only too much familiarity that will give the child the confidence to say that his father's penis is too small.

8. What else can one do for a mad brother except to provide him with rags?

9. You cannot be both taller and shorter than me.

10. Make sure your lover is good enough to be your wife should things get out of hand.

11. How can you describe an elephant to someone who has never seen one before?

12. A man cannot beget a male child before his father.

13. Knowledge is a luggage, each man carries his own.

14. It takes a small piece of cloth to make a dress for a small man.

15. Even the deaf need not be told that there is a riot in the market where he is.

16. My father said 'No matter how far you have gone in the wrong direction, turn back'.

17. Better search for the missing black goat while there is still light, for when it gets dark, it will be more difficult to find him.

18. There is no sense in shutting the barn door after the goat has escaped.

19. All fingers are not equal.

20. The cat buries its faeces for according to it; "before you know it what is rightly yours is being contested over."

21. Avoid a man who is content with a life of suffering.

22. If they call you a lion, be careful, for remember, the lion is also a wild animal.

23. Secrets are best kept within the family.

24. The monkey says, "yeah, I may not look so wonderful, but my mother loves me so."

25. Where the running man gets to, the man walking with determination will also eventually get there.

26. He who has seized something belonging to a child and raises up his arms so that the child can't reach it, when his arms begin to ache, he will bring it down and the child will take back what is his.

27. He who is holding his enemy to the ground is holding himself to the ground too.

28. The sheep lying on the ground is lying on its skin.

29. When a bachelor starts to moan and groan over his domestic chores, it is often an indication he has begun to think of marriage.

30. The animal that comes early to the water hole drinks clean water.

31. Someone who had been stung by a scorpion often jumps at the sight of a big ant.

32. Slow and steady is best for the journey that is life.

33. Alcohol says that it may look like water's cousin, but if it is mistreated or disrespected, then it will spring its surprises.

34. The earthworm that is stepped upon did not complain, but the man that stepped on it keeps moaning how the earthworm has soiled his foot.

35. In the morning when the antelope wakes up, he knows that he has to run faster than the fastest lion; otherwise he will end up as the lion's meal. In the morning when the lion wakes up he knows that he has to run faster than the slowest antelope; otherwise, he will starve to death. Therefore, when you wake up in the morning, whether you are a lion or an antelope, better start running.

36. A slap may be by impulse, but a knock on the head is obviously a deliberate action. *Soft words are the best cure for ill feelings.*

37. An open palm receives even more than it gives.

38. The heart of iron is broken with mere words

39. The tongue may be soft but it is a weapon that strikes fear into the mightiest.

40. The creator knows the power of the tongue, that is why He hides it inside the mouth, and puts the teeth in front of it to check its excesses.

41. When the poor man was told what it takes to become and remain rich, he opted to remain poor.

42. The man that always catches a thief at nights has to tell us what he does out late every night.

43. If the crocodile comes out from the deep sea and tells us that its mother has four eyes, there will be no grounds to enter into any arguments about this since none of us has been to the depth of the sea to see the crocodile's mother and count the number of eyes it has.

44. Whatever is holding the powerful man to the ground is more powerful than him as of that time.

45. If you think that education is expensive, then try illiteracy.

46. A wise child can differentiate between a wink and a blink.

47. A wise child needs not be told to come out from the scorching heat of the sun.

48. Twenty men can live harmoniously in a hut, until one of them gets married.

49. There is nothing the eyes can behold and weep out blood, instead of tears.

50. I am crazy, not stupid, a goat is a goat and a fool is a fool.

51. A thief comes as an enemy; a traitor comes as a friend.

52. It is only a greedy man that carries the meat of an entire elephant on his head, yet will be digging for crickets with his toes.

53. The delicious palm wine that could cause a quarrel between my best friend and I; may the calabash in which it is being carried break on its way to my home.

54. Never lend to a friend anything you cannot afford to give him as a gift.

55. The man who learnt that what he is about to borrow belongs to the local deity and changes his mind about borrowing it, never intended to return the item in the first place.

56. What else are friends for, if not to inconvenience one another?

57. A friend in need is a nuisance.

58. The problem is not marrying a beautiful woman; it is keeping her beautiful.

59. It is not the same expression that a man wears when he is borrowing that he also wears when he is returning the borrowed items or money.

Chris Dahi